by Wes Oleszewski

Avery Color Studios
Marquette, Michigan 49855
1993

ICE WATER MUSEUM

by Wes Oleszewski

Library of Congress Card #93-72739
ISBN #932212-78-6
First Edition December 1993
Reprinted 1996

Published
by Avery Color Studios
Marquette, Michigan 49855

Dedication

To Dave "Bullet" Willett

Table of Contents

Glossary

ABEAM—Beside, or perpendicular to the side of a vessel.

AFT—Behind, or to the rear of a vessel.

AGROUND—Running onto the bottom of shallow water.

BACK BROKEN—A vessel's hull fails across its width.

BALLAST—Something used to weigh a vessel down so that it runs lower in the water.

BARGE—A vessel that is intended to move cargo without power of its own.

BARK—Usually a three masted sailing vessel with mizzen-mast fore and aft rigged, and the others being square rigged (also known as a Barque).

BRIG—Two masted sailing vessel that is square rigged.

BULKHEAD—A vertical wall that divides the hull width-wise.

CANALLER—A vessel built specifically to transit the locks of the old Welland Canal.

CUT DOWN—To remove cabins and or decks to facilitate use of a vessel in another capacity.

DAVIT—The support boom normally used for swinging out and lowering lifeboats.

DONKEY BOILER—Used to produce steam for uses other than propulsion, such as steering and or heating.

FATHOM—Six feet.

FIRE HOLD—The portion of the engine room where crew-men stand and shovel coal into the furnace that heats the boilers.

FLOTSAM—Floating wreckage.

FO'C'SLE—The deck house built beneath the elevated portion of the bow (also known as fore castle).

FORE AND AFT RIGGED—Sails set parallel or lengthwise to the hull.

FOUNDER—To sink suddenly, or disastrously.

FUNNEL—Smoke stack.

GALE—Winds of between 40 and 74 miles per hour.

GUNNEL—(also known as gunwales) where the boat's side meets her spar deck.

HAWSER—A thick rope, or cable used for towing.

JIB-BOOM—Mast-like pole that extends forward from the peak of the bow.

KEEL—A beam running the length of the bottom of a vessel.

LIGHTER—To remove the cargo from a vessel, this name is sometimes attached to the vessel that the removed cargo is placed into.

LIST—Leaning to one side.

MIZZENMAST—The third mast back from the bow.

PEGGY—Shallow flat bottom boat similar to a rowboat or johnboat.

PORT SIDE—Left side.

SCHOONER-BARGE—Sailing vessel modified to be towed.

SCREW—Propeller.

SHOAL—Shallow area that creates a hazard.

SPAR—Mast.

SPAR DECK—The main deck through which the cargo is loaded.

STARBOARD—To the right hand side.

STEAM-BARGE—An early Great Lakes term meaning steamship, normally small, wooden and driven by propeller.

TEXAS DECK—The deck atop which the pilothouse is mounted.

YAWL—Small lifeboat, or rowboat.

Introduction

Anyone who has visited the Great Lakes and looked out upon the horizon to see one of the giant lake vessels crawling past, ponders about the kind of boat that it may be, where it is going and what it is carrying and what it is like to be aboard. Some people go a step beyond that and wonder about others that have passed long ago, and the people that sailed upon them. Their wonder is well placed, since all of the Great Lakes have a rich background of maritime adventure. Vessels and crews have challenged the lakes for a long, long time, with people making careers and living most of their lives on the freshwater seas. To all who open these pages, this text will be a small time-machine and with just a bit of imagination, the reader may be teleported back to witness the true-to-life adventures of some of the vessels and people who sailed the lakes, and have long since been forgotten. And the reader will be taken aboard a contemporary lakeboat to witness, first-hand, a December passage from Buffalo, New York to Superior, Wisconsin and back. I was there to learn the every-day workings and common jargon of a Great Lakes freighter in 1992.

Records show that more than 3,500 lakers have been lost on the five Great Lakes. The bottoms of the big lakes are littered with the remains of wooden schooners, sidewheel steamers, arched package freighters, iron and steel ore freighters of all kinds, many well-preserved in the cold dark depths. Undiscovered are the vast majority of these wrecks, waiting for decades and in many cases, centuries. The blue-green expanse of the Great Lakes is in essence an enormous ice water museum, where some of the exhibits are on open display, some are accessible to only a few visitors and most are waiting in the depths, forgotten or undiscovered. There are the overlooked adventures of the crews and boats that found themselves swept up into unusual or dangerous circumstances, but escaped to sail another day. Such adventures lay unremembered on rolls of micro-film and musty newspapers, at every city that once was called a port along the lake shores.

In this book the reader will be taken on a tour of the ice water museum, and along the way we will look into the obscure and often forgotten adventures of the vessels and people who have sailed the lakes. All of the stories told here are true and the chain of events that follow are recounted as best the author was able. In many cases, eye witness accounts of events as reported in the newspapers of the day were sourced to provide accuracy, while in other cases a pocket of facts were laid out and then logically interpolated between, to solve for a given result. When guess work was used, it has been noted, and occasional dialogue was manufactured for color. But for the most part, this book is an accurate historical narrative of the events.

With each diving season, research scuba divers seek and sometimes find long lost wrecks, and each time an author starts digging through old newspapers, a missing fact or two is stumbled upon. For this reason there is always the possibility of being in error when telling historical narratives such as this. Additionally, there are as many versions of the stories of lakeboats as there are tellers of these tales. Like any human, the author of this book can be wrong, but be assured that the best has been done to insure correctness. In my second book, for example, the name of a vessel master was taken from a number of sources, including newspapers and several books. It was only after the book was on the bookstore shelves that a prominent collector and historian informed me that the captain's name was spelled Payea and not "Payee" as had been sourced. The captain was a friend of the historian. To both, an apology, but such is the lot of writing books. It seems the corrections of these things come far too late to make the first edition, but I do the best I can do with what I have. When all is considered, this book is here for everyone, expert or casual boat watcher, to read, pick apart, ponder and enjoy.

Let us now climb aboard our time-tram and venture back to days past, getting to know people who long ago sailed the sky-colored seas that buoy up the giant steel freighters of today. This will be a visit to an exciting time, when the Great Lakes were the hub of the industrial revolution, or ruled by "king lumber." It is history lost and waiting for you, the reader, to find.

James Scallon's Embarrassment

Sullen was the atmosphere that hung over the State Street home of Captain George L. Stevens as a steady flow of relatives and friends began to arrive, intending to comfort his grieving widow. The sky was dull gray over Cleveland, and the fresh wind was still blowing hard from a bitter Lake Erie that seemed to reflect the spoiled sky. As this tainted Monday afternoon dragged toward a sorrow-filled evening, Chief Engineer Edward H. Stone and Mate John L. Andrews quietly entered the parlor of the Stevens home. Chief Stone tightly embraced his wife, who had been waiting there with Captain Stevens' spouse. The two ladies were close friends who had spent many a fine day sailing across the lakes on their husbands' boats, and many a storm-racked night seated near the fireplace conversing idly . . . and fearing the worst. Neither lady thought it would come to this, with one widowed and the other left with a survivor's guilt.

As the chief whispered quiet comfort to his wife, Mate Andrews shuffled quietly up to the gray-bearded pillar of a man who stood arrow straight, with hands locked at his lower back. The man was Harvey Stevens, Captain Stevens' father and owner of the boat his son mastered. Fiddling his hat nervously, with his eyes locked on the floor, Mate Andrews meekly reported to the owner, whose gaze was fixed over the sailor's head. "There was nothing we could do," he mumbled, "he said they may overload the yawl and he wouldn't get in . . . you know how he was . . . there was just nothing we could do." With a few brief heaves of his tight-vested chest the elder Stevens swallowed an approaching sob, for this was not the place nor the time for such emotion. Slowly the battered mate turned and melted into the thinning crowd . . . it was the 17th day of September, 1883.

Exactly one week before the sad gathering at the Stevens home, the 184 foot wooden steam-barge OAKLAND snored into the bustling freshwater port of Bay City, Michigan with Captain George Stevens in command. Coal, some 250 tons of it consigned to the P. C. Smith tug dock, was the steamer's burden and she was nearly two days late, having been weathered in at Sand Beach. Like most of her ilk, the OAKLAND had a long and complicated past, and even though the deck planking now below the Captain's feet was only 15 years old, the boat was considered to be one of the oldest on the lakes.

In the year 1840 at Erie, Pennsylvania the OAKLAND's roots were sprouted as the sidewheel passenger steamer MISSOURI. Less than three decades later, the once proud sidewheeler had fallen onto hard times and was abandoned at her port of birth where she soon sank and was left to rot. In 1867 Erie vessel builder William Loomis rowed his way over to the sad hulk of the MISSOURI and tromped aboard her lifeless deck. He had been considering the hulk for quite some time and had developed a plan to put it to profitable use.

By the first of the year Mr. Loomis had the sorry boat raised and put his shipwrights to work rebuilding the wreck into a propeller steam-barge for use in the lumber trade. By April of 1868 the new boat was launched, proudly bearing the name OAKLAND and measuring 184 feet long, 28 feet in beam and sporting a scant nine feet eight inches in depth. Her hull looked like that of a schooner with raised fo'c'sle and she had all of her cabins stacked aft with a tall hogging arch attached to each of her beams, supposedly to keep the boat from flexing. Although she appeared brand new when the Scott and Hearn interests bought her one month after her launch, the OAKLAND, in keeping with Great Lakes tradition, was considered as old as her original bottom from 1840.

For nearly a full decade the OAKLAND was in the gainful employ of Messrs. Scott and Hearn, until the summer of 1876 when she was sold to Buffalo vesselman John Ledger, and thus began a frenzy of exchanges in the OAKLAND's ownership. A month later she was sold to Samuel W. Gear, then half of her was bought by J.H. Tyler, who took total ownership the following year. By the end of the summer of 1878 Mitchael J. Galvin had her, but in September George F. Haywood had become her possessor. All of these owners were from Buffalo and all kept her in the lumber trade. In October 1878, as if to protest being passed around from one owner to another, the OAKLAND sank inside the port of Ashtabula, Ohio. Another Buffalo vesselman, Charles D. Marshall, bought her "as is where is," and returned her to her toil. At length, in March of 1880, the family Stevens of Cleveland purchased the boat and she seemed once again to have found a home. By her September 10th, 1883 arrival at Bay City, all aboard the vessel were quite comfortable.

Snorting horses tugged at the block and tackle that lifted the giant buckets of coal from the OAKLAND's hold. The dockside pile grew slowly near the P.C. Smith tug company's office shanty and before long the OAKLAND would be off to the nearby Chamberlin lumber dock for her outbound cargo. Since the beginning of the month the weather had been a mixture of rude and nasty, but now appeared to be showing signs of improvement. By Tuesday evening the OAKLAND was emptied of her coal cargo and hissed over to the Chamberlin dock. Quickly the dock-wollopers went to work loading the lumber aboard her, one board at a time.

Bay City being a regular stop in the OAKLAND's work was just fine for a number of her crew. Chief Engineer Stone, his Second Engineer Robert Hanna, Mate Andrews and Wheelsman Montgomery were all from the port city, so the steamer's frequent arrivals into the Saginaw River allowed abundant opportunity to visit home. Such opportunities were rare for other members of the OAKLAND's crew, particularly deckhand Thomas Halligan of Springfield, Illinois and Thomas O'Rourke who was from Paterson, New Jersey. For these men the boat was their home from the time the ice began to break across the lakes until it locked the channels again nearly nine months later.

As Wednesday's loading proceeded Mate Andrews strode across the gangway and headed directly for Captain Stevens. By keeping his ears open, the resourceful mate had caught wind of a loaded barge that happened to be heading the OAKLAND's way and was in need of a convenient tow. Considering that the OAKLAND's destination was the Carroll Brothers lumber dock in Erie and that the waiting barge was bound for the Bell lumber dock at Cleveland, a tow for cash would be in the interest of both vessels. Mate Andrews was promptly sent to the schooner-barge to close the deal.

With 355,000 board feet of lumber tucked in her hold and high upon her deck, the OAKLAND departed the Chamberlin dock and pushed her way to the Mason dock where the 162 foot schooner-barge GEORGE W. WESLEY squatted with 425,000 board feet between her three tall masts. In short order the towing hawser was made fast between the two, and Captain Stevens gave Wheelsman Charles Dickson the word to steer through the draws and bring the pair onto Saginaw Bay. Also traveling at the favor of the OAKLAND were the wives of both Captain Stevens and Chief Stone. Mrs. Stevens had been aboard for some time, making a pleasure trip, and while the OAK-

Built on the bones of the side wheeler MISSOURI, the OAKLAND was kept busy hauling bulk cargos and lumber. Having had a number of owners, the boat became a common sight on the lower lakes. This drawing is the author's concept of how she may have looked.

LAND had been working in Bay City she had convinced her friend Mrs. Stone to join her. Such trips by the spouses of vesselmen were quite common on the lakes and both ladies often had been aboard the boat.

Departing across Saginaw Bay, the OAKLAND and her consort were exceptions to what was currently a slump in the normally booming lumber industry, the problem being primarily a lack of available vessels to haul lumber. Prices in the iron ore and particularly the grain trade had risen to the point where an estimated one third of the lumber fleet was now engaged in hauling these commodities. So, the departure of the OAKLAND and WESLEY along with that of the PASSAIC and her consort barge ELMA, as well as the steamer S.D. CALDWELL and her string of barges, COMMODORE, STAR OF HOPE and HATTIE, were only a fraction of the lumber traffic that normally marched from the Saginaw River on a given day. When the barge SYLVIA MORTON headed out for Toledo, the dock wollopers waited idly for the next hull to be stacked. Most were paid their share and simply strolled the waterfront waiting for the whistle of the next steamer tooting for the draws. That day only four steamers, the P.H. BIRKHEAD, GERMANIA, A.A. TURNER and MAYFLOWER, plus the barge J.R. EDWARDS, reported in the river—not nearly enough work to go around.

Unsettled would best describe the weather that met the lakeboats on their outbound trek. Clouds that were billowing white swept across an abnormally deep blue sky, and a blustery cold bitter wind puffed down from the northeast. Every time that it seemed the autumn sun was out to stay the clouds began to bunch together once again and cast an indifferent shadow over the scene. With billows of coal smoke streaking from her tall skinny funnel, the OAKLAND pointed her wooden bow into Saginaw Bay's chop. The distance up the bay is just over 50 miles and required the lumber boats to thread the shallows between Sand Point and the Charity Islands. Having passed safely up across the bay Captain Stevens arced the two boats around the tip of Michigan's thumb and headed down Lake Huron.

Through the night's passage downbound, the weather grew rude and the OAKLAND started to corkscrew in the following sea. From the OAKLAND's octagon pilothouse Captain Stevens tapped knowingly at the ship's barometer, for another nasty bit of weather appeared to be in the making. By dawn the entrance to the St. Clair River was in sight and the shelter of Port Huron widened to welcome the OAKLAND. Riding with the swift current, the steamer and her consort eased up along the west shore and tied up at the Black River entrance. With his eye to the weather, Captain Stevens had decided hours before that the two ladies should be put safely ashore as soon as the boat could fix a gangplank. They would continue on by train. Mrs. Stevens would set out for the family home in Cleveland and Mrs. Stone had decided to keep her company instead of heading back for west Bay City. Perhaps if the weather moderated, the engineer's wife could catch the OAKLAND back home in her husband's company when the boat returned the following week. The wives stood dockside and waved as the OAKLAND creaked off downbound and vanished along the bending river.

In the first hours of Sunday morning the OAKLAND and WESLEY cleared the Detroit River, and Lake Erie met the pair with an ill temper, but not the storm that Captain Stevens had been expecting. After successfully zigzagging through Pelee Passage's treachery, the lumber-laden duo turned on a 120 degree course for Cleveland. By suppertime Sunday, the OAKLAND drew near Cleveland as deckhands O'Rourke and Halligan emerged from cook Ed Davis' galley, picking their teeth and trailing thick dinner aromas. With no fanfare at all the OAKLAND's towing hawser was let loose and taken up by the deckhands, thus delivering her barge. Mate Andrews, who had been watching from the boat deck, gave the word to press on ahead, and in a belch of black smoke the schooner-barge G.W. WESLEY was imparted as agreed. The two deckhands vanished again into the galley and the OAKLAND headed on toward the port of Erie.

Just as the OAKLAND passed Ashtabula, Ohio, the barometer began to drop rapidly, as a wind out of the northwest began to stiffen. The storm that Captain Stevens had anticipated was suddenly upon the boat and had found her in an unfortunate position. Running along the exposed south shore, the OAKLAND was quickly subjected to sharp waves that had been building across the width of Lake Erie. Asleep in his cabin, Captain Stevens was awakened by the trespassing lake when it began to come in below the doorway and warped foundation. Gathering what dry bed gear he could manage, the frustrated master sloshed his way down the companionway and sought out the cabin door of Chief Stone. "You mind if I sleep in your cabin?" he asked, clutching his blanket, pillow and gaunt mattress like a kid in search of a slumber party, "Mine's leakin' again." Motioning for the captain to pull up some floor and make himself at home, the chief grunted a drowsy approval. The chief's quarters were more water-resistant than those of the master and the door was on the starboard side, so it was in lee of the superstructure. No sooner had Captain Stevens rolled off his socks and shoved his cold toes beneath the sheets than he was fast asleep. The OAKLAND rolled on into the fitful night.

A sudden loud crash, as if a cartload of crockery had been dumped upon the deck, shocked Captain Stevens and Chief Stone back to consciousness. Stumbling over one another the two men bounded on deck in a comical panic, each clad only in their underalls. Rounding the fantail, they were met with a torrent of wreckage. The waves had demolished the entire port side of the deckhouse and the OAKLAND had now taken on a list. Out in the darkness the seas had started to run very high, taking advantage of the aged steamer. Wading among the broken cabins, steward Davis was attempting in vain to gather the scattered tools of his missing galley. Stumbling back to the chief's quarters, the captain and engineer pulled on pants and socks, captain grabbing a thick overcoat. The boat was in critical condition—they had only minutes to save her.

Taking command in the pilothouse, the captain ordered most of the deckload thrown overboard, in an attempt to overcome the list, while the chief stormed down to the firehold to rule over the pumps. Both efforts did little to save the OAKLAND, for Lake Erie had her and was not about to let go. The missing cabins left the companionways vulnerable to the boarding waves, and the water swirled down into the fire-hole. Steeply the OAKLAND rolled, as numb-handed crewmen tossed board after board of her cargo into the lake. Like a pot boiling over, sooty steam burst from below the boat's decks. Fireman Fred Hart, followed by the chief engineer, fought his way from the engine room. Lake Erie had penetrated Chief Stone's domain and snuffed the OAKLAND's fires. Now the battered wooden lakeboat rolled at the mercy of the storm.

Shortly before five o'clock in the morning the OAKLAND's list had become so severe that it became difficult to stand on her deck. The seas were boarding her constantly and the resulting rolls had started to shift the deck cargo about. From side to side the planks of lumber were slung, until they had bludgeoned out her framework and smashed the cross-beams from her tall arches. As the crew tried in vain to quell the chaos on the cargo deck, Lake Erie rose up and demolished the after deck. For Captain Stevens this signaled the end of his command—he ordered the crew to take to the yawl and abandon ship.

In modern times, crews who sail the lakes are equipped with self-inflating covered life rafts and lifeboats with the capacity for 50 persons, but in the storm-racked pre-dawn hours of September 17th, 1883 those aboard the stricken OAKLAND were in possession of no such luxuries. The tiny wooden yawl in which they were attempting their escape could be best described as nothing more than a rowboat. Into the yawl piled Thomas O'Rourke, Fred Hart, Thomas Halligan, Harry Montgomery, Ed Davis, Watchman John Farrington, and Chief Stone. As First Mate Andrews struggled to board the boat, Captain Stevens could easily see that the boat was greatly overloaded and flatly refused to leave the OAKLAND. Wheelsman Charles Dickson, Second Engineer Robert Hanna and Fireman John Glosson all felt their chances were far better on the wallowing OAKLAND than in the yawl. Captain Stevens was not a man to argue with and his order for Mate Andrews to shove off with the overburdened lifeboat was final. Standing at the OAKLAND's rail the four stay-behinds watched as the yawl was tossed into the darkness, some men rowing, the rest bailing.

Nearly two hours passed between the time the yawl departed and the end came for the OAKLAND. The gray dawn had come as the decks beneath the four who remained suddenly began to go to pieces, and the steamer started her death plunge. Captain Stevens saw that he was in for some swimming and quickly rid himself of his overcoat. A moment later the boat's deck burst upward with escaping air, as Lake Erie swallowed the OAKLAND stern first.

Until half past nine that morning, the castaways rowed and bailed the yawl. Finally the sad lot reached the protected waters of Conneaut, Ohio and reported the loss of the OAKLAND. News dispatches and speculation as to the boat's foundering spread like brush fire. In their haste to get the story out, the local reporters even went so far as to make up names for crewmen. That afternoon the "Cleveland Herald" ran a story quoting James Scallon, a simple clerk in the marine business, who had been bellowing up and down the waterfront that the OAKLAND was "loaded right down to her decks being under water." How this Cleveland clerk had come by this apparently damning information was never made clear. At the time that mattered little because it was enough to fire the furnace of wild speculation and blame.

Those who would point the finger of blame for the loss of the vessel, of course, aimed directly at Captain Stevens. How handy it is to have a dead captain, who can not speak up in his defense, to pin the loss of a vessel on. The speculation now ran wild. The boat was said not only to be overloaded, but was called unseaworthy and accused of having to shelter whenever the slightest weather came up. That was why, according to the media, the captain had put the ladies off at Black River and why the OAKLAND was forced to shelter at Sand Beach on the way up. Yes, indeed there was plenty of nasty blame to heap upon the late Captain Stevens!

Throughout that Monday, rumors and speculation caused as great a storm in Cleveland as the one blowing in from the lake. Those gathering at Captain Stevens' State Street home had no idea that the stubborn master was alive and well and drifting on a piece of the OAKLAND's shattered deck. Also clinging to the 12 by 20 foot hunk of flotsam were the three other members of the crew who had stayed aboard the OAKLAND. All around the four men the lake heaved up waves of ice water spiked with sharp-cornered lumber. Every wave that broke over the shivering survivors brought bruising boards pounding down upon them. To make matters worse, the stray lumber threatened to beat their makeshift raft to bits, so the men took turns fending off the boards. Two at a time, the men would shield the others until they were too tired to work, then the other two would take over. It was a draining rotation that kept a pair of the men kneeling atop the raft and the others in the water. In the distance the four men could see tugs searching about three miles off shore, but the survivors were bobbing among the waves some five miles farther out in the lake.

Into a premature dusk the hours dragged as the exhausted quartet continued to take turns on and off the raft. They knew too well that the coming of darkness meant that the search efforts would be suspended and that there was the good chance that some—or all—of them might not survive the cold night to see the following day. Along the south horizon the amber lights of Conneaut glowed as if to further torment the unfortunate four. For what seemed like endless numb hours of pitch-black darkness, they fought off sleep—to fall asleep would invite hypothermia and death.

In the pre-dawn darkness the four beaten survivors spied the government steamer HAZE pushing through the now-wide field of floating lumber, heading directly toward the castaways. Their hearts soared and their strength was renewed. Quickly, their numb hands gathered the signaling equipment that they had been saving. Two unusual items were at hand, a whistle and a pistol, and the men used both of them to try to attract the attention of the HAZE. As the steamer passed within 500 feet of the men, they saw someone walking out on deck with a lantern. The castaways shouted at the top of their lungs, blew the whistle and fired the pistol, but the HAZE went past and continued on her downbound course.

Dawn found the four men beaten and tired, but alive in spite of Lake Erie. At 7 o'clock Tuesday morning the tug PERRY sailed right up to the castaways, as if she had known all along where they were, and the four were plucked from the lake's grip. The problem had been that the jettisoned deckload had formed a field far south of the actual wreckage, and this first area had been mistaken as the one and only wreckage left by the OAKLAND and was searched fruitlessly by the tugs on Monday. By Tuesday the northwest wind had blown the main field close enough for the tug PERRY to stumble upon. No sooner had the tug started toward the flotsam than the men were spotted.

By mid-day Captain Stevens had recovered to the point where he was ready to go before the press and answer the charges against him. Much to the embarrassment of his detractors, he pointed out the fact that the OAKLAND carried an insurance rating of B2, which was nominal for a boat of her age and construction. And when the OAKLAND took shelter at Sand Beach she was in the company of a fleet of lakeboats which included such staunch vessels as the DON M. DICKINSON, GEORGE KING, ROBERT HOLLAND, PORTER CHAMBERLIN, BAY CITY and C.F. CURTIS, all of whom were newer and more powerful than the OAKLAND. The masters of these boats had found the weather severe enough to shelter, so why should the antiquated OAKLAND be accused of being "tender" for sheltering? Finally, there was the matter of the overloading. On three different occasions Captain Stevens and the OAKLAND had taken cargos of 371,000 board-feet, which was 16,000 board feet more than she had on at the time of her sinking. In fact, her fender rails were all out of the water, which would be several feet from being anywhere near "overloaded." The captain's words were printed on Wednesday and those who revel in accusations, rumors and unsubstantiated claims were abruptly silenced. There was in particular one loud-spoken clerk who was highly embarrassed when the lost captain came back to life. Clerk James Scallon faded into obscurity and was never quoted by the newspapers again.

Surrounded by floating lumber, the OAKLAND was found with four feet of her bow sticking straight up out of the water. In the weeks that followed, the boat's owners hired the steamer GEORGE A. MARSH to gather up what remained of the floating cargo. On the 25th of September, 1883, the remains of the OAKLAND were sold to James Corrigan and wreck diver Captain Thomas Wilson for $500. Their plan was said to be to drag the hulk ashore, salvage what cargo was trapped in her hold and either salvage her engine works if possible, or rebuild her if she was worth it. There is no record of either action—only the fact that her enrollment was surrendered on September 30th, 1883 and endorsed as "vessel sunk and abandoned."

Perhaps because she was unable, or unwilling, to drown any of her crew, or perhaps because of the misplaced speculation concerning the sinking, the wreck of the OAKLAND faded from the marine columns nearly as fast as clerk James Scallon. Today the OAKLAND has long been forgotten and just possibly the boisterous clerk's embarrassment has faded as well.

The Rites of Spring

Every year there is a single event that marks winter's passing from the Great Lakes. For some it is the sight of the first robin, or the sounds of free running water in a thawed creek, or perhaps even the start of hockey playoffs. At Sault Saint Marie ("the Soo"), it is the appearance of the first oreboat of the season at the Soo locks. In modern times the first boat will crush its way around Mission Point upbound, making the required radio report to Soo Control and the Lock Master, " . . . up at the Mission." Coast Guard ice breakers assist today's giants as they overcome the frozen Saint Marys River, pushing past the still-closed tour boat docks and the snoozing VALLEY CAMP museum ship. Occasionally, a boat from the upper lakes will do the honors, opening the season with a downbound cargo. With little fanfare the first boat of the season will work its way against the floes of pack ice and through the lock. Normally, this scene is acted out in the third week of March and with the aid of modern radio communications the whole event is forecast well in advance and little is left to risk.

In 1909 the situation was quite different. The ice had the lakes in its frozen grip until April, and powerful ice breakers such as the modern MACKINAW had yet to be invented, so the oreboats did not start moving until the end of the month. At the port town of Sault Saint Marie, most of the residents made their living from the fleet of lakers and their crews. Each boat that tied up at the locks, waiting its turn, gave those aboard a chance to go ashore and pick up an item or two that would make life aboard ship a bit more pleasant. When winter closed navigation, the local merchants were left with far fewer patrons than during the season. There would be at least four lean months before the boats and the money that their crews carried would return.

Telegraph information from the lower lakes to the Soo had been hinting that the boats in the lower lakes were breaking out. From Toronto, came word that the Mutual and Merchants Navigation Company's canaller HADDINGTON was departing for the Soo, along with the Canadian Lake Line's canaller J.H. PLUMMER. Word from Cleveland said that the Union Steamship Company's 256 foot canal steamer GLENELLAH was on the way up, with the canallers BEAVERTON and HAMILTON. Additionally, the word was out that Gilchrist's C.H. WATSON was due at De Tour at any time, along with C.W. Elphicke's 376 foot steel oreboat G. WATSON FRENCH. Like the FRENCH, the package steamers NORTHERN WAVE and NORTHERN LIGHT were due in the lower St. Marys River bound from Milwaukee. The lake fleet was stirring to life and the residents and shopkeepers of the Soo could not have been happier.

On Sunday April 18, 1909, the NORTHERN WAVE, NORTHERN LIGHT and G. WATSON FRENCH arrived at De Tour and the following morning all three set out, "bucking the ice" to the Soo. Through the entire day the three made less than two miles with the NORTHERN WAVE and NORTHERN LIGHT turning back while still within sight of De Tour. The FRENCH made it as far as four and a half miles to Sweets Point, but that took until one o'clock in the afternoon. Captain W.W. Eger decided at that point that if he were to get back to De Tour before dark, he had best turn there and head back. The ice below Lime Island, Captain Eger reckoned, was piled upon itself 14 inches thick.

Through the evening the officers of the FRENCH schemed against the ice and came up with a plan that just might give the boat an advantage. As much ballast as possible would be pumped into the steamer's aft tanks, lifting her bow nearly out of the water. The big steel steamer would ride up on top of the ice and the boat's own weight would crush a path of open water. At dawn on Tuesday the FRENCH, sporting her new posture, started once more up the St. Marys. This time she smashed through the ice at Lime Island in less than an hour and by four o'clock in the afternoon she rounded Mission Point and hauled toward the locks. Ashore, expectant residents waved and shouted from the riverbank, and the FRENCH responded with a four-toot whistle salute. Other whistles from the land along the St. Marys rang a responding ditto to the steamer's salute. Soon every piece of equipment whose whistle had steam available was hooting a joyful greeting to the first boat of the season. Crunching up to the north pier of the Poe lock, the FRENCH was boarded by a happy mob of local vesselmen and dignitaries. Captain Eger was interviewed by the press, greeted by the community leaders and, at a quarter to seven in the evening, proceeded through the lock. Behind the FRENCH came the NORTHERN WAVE, and the NORTHERN LIGHT, all of whom snugged up to the wall above the locks and put out lines to await the dawn and their chance to buck the ice to Lake Superior. With less fanfare, four Canadian boats passed upbound during the night and tied up above, making certain that the Soo was again open for business.

Four days after the G. WATSON FRENCH's triumphant opening of the Soo, the big steamer, along with the NORTHERN WAVE and the NORTHERN LIGHT, was still at the lock wall waiting to proceed. With them, however, were the lakeboats SUPERIOR, SONORA, YOSEMITE, SULTANA, NORTHERN KING, NORTH WIND, JAMES S. DUNHAM, SEHUYLKILL, CODORUS and ROCHESTER. Waiting below the locks was another fleet of lakers impatient to start the season, the GEORGE N. NESTER, SUPERIOR CITY, WILLIAM E. COREY, WARD AMES, MAHONING, GEORGE F. BAKER, J.S. KEEFE, ELBERT H. GARY, S.N. PARENT and JOHN LAMBERT. On the Canadian side waited the MIDLAND PRINCE, MIDLAND KING, WAHCONDAH, NEEBING, NEEPEWAH, STRATHCONA, WESTMOUNT, GLENMOUNT, FAIRMOUNT, STORMOUNT, GLENELLAH, CITY OF MONTREAL, ADVANCE and SCOTTISH HERO, with two barges. All were trapped at the Soo by heavy ice that had piled up at Point Iroquois some 15 steaming miles above the locks, effectively blocking the passage to Lake Superior. Below the locks, the river was relatively clear, and the boats had started to pile up at the port. Making matters worse, the steamer PALIKI was loading rails at the Commercial dock in preparation to head up to Port Arthur and as soon as she cleared the LEAFIELD was going to take her place and do the same. At the same dock the AGAWA was unloading coal and would join the crowd when she finished. To add to the traffic jam, there were a score of vessels upbound from the lower lakes with no inkling of the 44 boat blockade at the Soo.

Among the crowd of soon-to-be-stuck upbounders was a rather unremarkable vessel that easily could be overlooked among the snarl of lakeboats struggling to begin the season. Under the command of Captain Robert C. Pringle, the red-hulled steamer AURANIA sauntered into the lower St. Marys River at dawn on Sunday April 25, 1909, and headed up to the Soo. Shortly before noon the AURANIA pressed around Mission Point. From the lookout tower the ship reporter shouted via his megaphone that the upper river was blocked by ice but boats could still lock upbound. Captain Pringle responded with a wave of his hand as the AURANIA continued on her way.

The AURANIA herself, although somewhat ordinary by sight, had an interesting background. Launched in 1895

COURTESY MILWAUKEE PUBLIC LIBRARY MARINE COLLECTION

Converted from a barge, the AURANIA retained her square lines. She proved to be no match for the ice off Isle Parisienne in 1909.

at the Chicago Shipbuilding Company, she originally came out as a steel schooner-barge measuring 364 feet long, 40 feet in beam and 26 feet in depth. Officers quarters and the pilothouse were stacked upon her spar deck behind her number one hatchway, and crew quarters were divided between the standard aft deck house located over her stern and a "dog house" that was set amidships. The AURANIA sported three elegantly raked spars, one ahead the forward deck house, the second planted behind the dog house and the third just ahead of the aft quarters. Those spars were an eye-pleasing contrast to the boat's boxy hull, constructed without the curving sheer of most vessels of her era. This type of construction, known as "straightback" on the three vessels that were actually designed as such, was a passing fad that influenced many vessels built in the mid 1890s. An arresting feature of the AURANIA was the fact that she had no lifeboat rigging atop her aft deck house. Instead, the two yawls were attached to the ends of the booms that extended from each of her foremost spars. Apparently, it was planned that in case of emergency the life boats could be simply swung over the side and lowered from the boom. Such cost-effective short cuts marked this economy class lakeboat.

Demands for more steamers to feed the industrial revolution prompted the AURANIA's return to Chicago just four years after her launching, for conversion to a propeller-driven steamer at the Ship Owner's Dry Dock Company. All that was altered in the boat's appearance was that the smokestack for her donkey boiler was replaced with a larger funnel appropriate for the new steam engine. Her masts were shifted to clear the way for the newer unloading rigs with the fore mast being set behind the forward quarters and the after mast eliminated altogether. To make room for the additional crew needed to work a steamer, her aft quarters were expanded. Now the new AURANIA could work on her own or even tow a barge if her owners so dictated.

Shortly after clearing Mission Point, Captain Pringle got a much better idea of the scope of the oreboat blockade near the locks. More than 50 lakers sat with their beams tied one to another waiting for the chance to pass upbound. The spring air hung heavy around the brooding lakers with the sooty coal smoke that trickled from their funnels. Through the crowd, the AURANIA picked her way and nosed into the Poe lock. Passing up at ten minutes after one o'clock in the afternoon, the coal-laden steamer headed past the blockaded fleet and up the river. The ice met her at about Point Aux Pins and with a rumble the shattered frozen surface of the St. Marys River gave way ahead of the AURANIA's bluff bow.

Unlike the people who managed the lake vessels, the merchants at the Soo were delighted by the oreboat blockade. The town was filled with roaming sailors and the stores and particularly the saloons were doing a booming business. It was as if the Soo had been transformed from a hibernating village to a marine boom town overnight. In this, the era before security fences along the locks, people were in the habit of strolling aboard the tied-up lakeboats. This meant that the moored vessels were a fertile opportunity for every carpet-bagging door-to-door salesman and huckster that could reach the Soo. The result was that the boats were crawling with uninvited guests. In response to this problem, the captain of the Steel Trust boat SUPERIOR CITY allegedly came up with a tasteless—but effective—solution.

Early Monday morning, Dr. Griffin, the local health officer at the American Soo, started to get visitors asking what to do about the smallpox quarantine that his office had issued. There followed a number of phone calls inquiring as to which boats tied up at the locks Dr. Griffin had quarantined. The news puzzled the good doctor, who had issued no quarantine order and certainly knew nothing about any outbreak of smallpox. By noon Dr. Griffin had heard enough. Scooping up his doctor's satchel and plopping on his derby, he headed to the locks to see for himself. Upon reaching the locks he started asking around, but found that most people had only heard rumors. The arrival of the health officer at the locks now added fuel to the wildfire rumor and it began to spread faster than any infectious disease could. A couple of the lockmen said that they had heard that the SUPERIOR CITY had been displaying a smallpox sign for a few hours the previous evening, and this gave the doctor a direction to point his investigation. Armed with that information he made his way to the upper south pier where the SUPERIOR CITY was tied up. Stomping up the wooden rung ladder, the doctor boarded the boat and demanded to speak to the vessel's master. There followed a short and somewhat heated conference in which everyone Dr. Griffin spoke to denied having any knowledge of any smallpox sign. With a stern warning that any misuse of a contagious disease sign would be immediately reported to the Michigan Secretary of State, Dr. Griffin made his way back down the ladder. As the health officer headed toward Portage Avenue, the SUPERIOR CITY's captain and mate exchanged a slight smirk. In the ensuing days there were far fewer uninvited guests aboard any of the boats, especially the SUPERIOR CITY.

At first light Tuesday morning the 27th, many of the boats that had been tied up at the Soo cast off their lines and started upbound. There had been little change in the ice conditions at Point Iroquois, but nearly 40 boats departed to attempt passage. The motivation behind such a futile exodus was not a burning desire to load or deliver cargo, nor was it the urge to make money—it was simply the desire of captains and management to outfox labor. The Lake Seamen's Union had widely publicized that their negotiations with the vessel owners affiliated with the Lake Carriers Association were going badly and their 10,000 members could be expected to walk off their boats on a general strike before the end of the week. The wily captains knew that it would be much more difficult to walk off a lakeboat that was stuck in the ice than one tied to the lock wall. So the boats headed out fully expecting to get stuck less than 15 miles above the Soo.

Ahead of the departing fleet, Captain Pringle and the AURANIA had already had a rather touchy entanglement with the ice. From Point Aux Pins the steamer had smashed her way upbound against increasingly rigid ice conditions. As the steamer worked near Bay Mills, the pressure of the floes on the starboard side was clearly increasing and it seemed the AURANIA was being forced toward shore. After an agonizing struggle, the ice got the better of the steamer and forced the AURANIA aground. Luckily the boat had only touched the bottom and was not firmly snagged. After a fair amount of swearing and an equal amount of backing and turning, the AURANIA managed to pull herself free and began to shove toward Whitefish Bay.

South of the AURANIA's struggle, the impatient fleet had also started to do battle with the ice. Unknown to the boats slugging it out on the river that day, a fierce spring gale was charging across Lake Superior at that very moment and was bearing down on the preoccupied lakeboats. A sudden northwest wind erupted, screaming—and swallowed Whitefish Bay and the Soo whole. Lakes Superior, Michigan and Huron were whipped into a simultaneous frenzy, squalls of snow spitting across the region. Along the lock wall at the Soo the Steel Trust boats, which had been given instructions by the owners not to buck ice this season, put out extra lines and waited, thankful to be in port.

Onboard the AURANIA, Captain Pringle had no desire to fight a spring storm, and as luck would have it the winds had blown the ice southwest, opening the water between him and Isle Parisienne. Without a moment's hesitation he ran his boat for the lower end of the island and the shelter that the island's mass provided. As the AURANIA seemed within reach of the island, Captain Pringle, Wheelsman William Hocking and Second Mate L.W. Nordeman watched in subdued horror as the wind brought the ice toward the boat once more, this time from both sides. Long before the steamer could reach the lee of Isle Parisienne the charging ice slammed against her beam and, aided by the wind, shoved her into the other pack. The whole trap started to carry the AURANIA southeast toward Gros Cap on the Canadian shore. For a while it appeared as if the frozen vise would ground the steamer

COURTESY MILWAUKEE PUBLIC LIBRARY MARINE COLLECTION

From the pilot house window of the submarine decker GEORGE W. PEAVEY, Captain Boyce watched helplessly as the crew of the AURANIA abandoned ship. Locked tightly in the ice near the PEAVEY, Captain Randall did the same from the FREDERICK B. WELLS, twin to the PEAVEY.

for a second time. But just as she was approaching dangerous waters, the winds swung around to the east and the frigid clamp holding the AURANIA opened, exposing a path toward Isle Parisienne's elusive shelter. Captain Pringle worked his steamer along the narrow gap toward shelter. Forcing the AURANIA as far as the ice would allow, the boat's master finally gave up and settled for what shelter he could get. The sun set Wednesday night with the AURANIA several miles short of Isle Parisienne.

Through the night the wind shifted more toward the southeast and crammed the AURANIA into the thickest of the ice once again, this time just below the island. Captain Pringle sensed the nearing possibility of fetching up on Isle

Parisienne. As dawn approached he resumed the duel with the ice, working as best he could toward the west, but the steel laker came to a grinding stop as her bow crunched into a windrow. A series of backing and charging maneuvers were started, and at half past seven Thursday morning she appeared to be working her way free. About that same time, the captain sent First Mate McLaren up to the fore peak to check on the condition of the bow plates under the stress of the ice buckling. The mate reported back that all was in order and the captain ordered another charge at the ice. A moment later the deck beneath their feet lurched as the boat rolled so heavily that for an agonizing moment all aboard thought the AURANIA was going to keep going and capsize on the spot. Just as suddenly as she started to roll, the motion stopped, leaving the steamer with a severe list. Instinctively the captain rang full reverse and a long moment later the steamer churned backward in the short channel she had just cut, and piled up under full power on the heavy ice at the other end.

After a quick inspection, Chief Cleveland found an intimidating amount of water coming in below, but from where he could not tell. Starting the pumps, the chief sent word up to Captain Pringle that the boat had opened her plates somewhere. With that report, Captain Pringle dispatched hands to help in pumping and others of the crew to seek out the leak. For more than an hour the AURANIA's crew searched frantically, but could not find the source of the intruding water. By nine a.m. it had become painfully obvious that the water had overtaken the pumps, because the AURANIA continued to settle steadily. Captain Pringle ordered the boat's whistle continuously blown in a distress signal. There were several big oreboats in the distance and the urgent echoes of the AURANIA's whistle would doubtless bring them smashing to the rescue through the ice floes.

For the better part of the next hour the AURANIA was slowly swallowed by Whitefish Bay, as her whistles of distress rolled across the frozen water. But the distant lakeboats that Captain Pringle had been so certain would speed to his rescue just sat there in the distance, like tin cut-outs at a carnival shooting gallery. There were no billows of coal smoke from their tall stacks, no puffs of steam from their whistles and no change in their position at all. Captain Pringle came to a solitary and lonely conclusion... there was no help coming. With the AURANIA groaning and beginning to list even more severely beneath the crew, the boat's master made the decision that every captain avoids thinking about—the decision to abandon the boat.

Abandoning the AURANIA would have been less complicated on the open lake in a gale of wind. The crew could go over the side, but the lifeboats were designed to be rowed across open water not the frozen surface of the bay. Now they were swung out on the booms and used to drop the crew to the ice. Frenzied feet clopped across the boat's deck as personal possessions were gathered in haste, and with what little of their holdings the crew could gather, they started over the side one by one. The thick ice that the boat's stern had piled onto now supported her, allowing a bit of extra time for her people to escape. Departing his charge, Captain Pringle took a final head count—there were 19 including himself, one man short. Conspicuously absent from the crowd on the ice was Chief Cleveland, apparently still occupied in the lost cause of working the boat's pumps. Mate McLaren was sent below with orders to drag the chief up on deck if need be.

Unknown to the ice-borne refugees, their plight had not gone unnoticed by the distant boats. There were a number of eyes focused on them through binoculars the whole time. From the pilothouses of two downbound submarine deckers, the GEORGE W. PEAVEY and FREDER-

COURTESY MILWAUKEE PUBLIC LIBRARY MARINE COLLECTION

For two and one half hours, the crew of the AURANIA hiked over the ice in an effort to get to the J.H. BARTOW, seen here on a better day.

ICK B. WELLS, the dilemma of the AURANIA's people was being observed with helpless frustration. Onboard the PEAVEY, Captain L.C. Boyce was leaning out of the open pilothouse window with his elbows planted firmly on the sill to support the binoculars he had pressed to his eyes for the better part of the last hour. The captain had heard the AURANIA's distress signals loud and clear, but his boat was trapped firmly in the grip of the heavy ice. Now the abrupt ending of the taunting distress signals could mean only one thing. The AURANIA was at her end. Across the four miles of ice that stretched between the PEAVEY and the AURANIA, Captain Boyce watched as the stricken crew went over the side. "Blast!" he whispered into the emptiness between the boats as he lowered the binoculars from his face slightly, "they're goin' over now." For just a moment he put himself in the place of the other master, then went back to peering through the lenses like a helpless spectator. The rest of the pilothouse crew stood still and silent with their attention divided between their captain and the distant sinking vessel, wondering what, if anything, the "old man" was going to do to help. But there was nothing that he could do. His boat was welded into the ice.

Close behind the PEAVEY, Captain Randall of the WELLS was watching with equal helplessness. Neither of the masters could make out the name of the luckless boat, but her color and profile suggested it was one of the Corrigan fleet and probably the AURANIA. Her crew now started the imperilled trek across the ice toward safety. Unfortunately for Captain Randall, the flock of castaways was headed away from his boat.

Once Captain Pringle had his crew gathered on the ice, he had a difficult decision to make. They could head for Isle Parisienne, which was only a few thousand feet to the north, but with the prevailing ice conditions it could be mid-May before anyone could rescue them. In Captain Pringle's mind, no matter how he looked at it, that option could mean a long time eating pigeons and drinking lakewater! The only logical path to safety was across the jumble of plate ice to the lakeboats in the distance. Thrown up in tall ridges in some places and split open revealing open water in others, the trip would be a dangerous one at best. To increase their chances, the crew decided to drag both lifeboats and a small skiff, or "peggy boat" with them. Shoving the two big lifeboats over the first bit of distance and the first ridge or so convinced the castaways that they were simply too heavy a burden. With great relief, the crewmen assigned to lugging the lifeboats left them behind and dragging only the peggy, caught up to the others.

Nearest to the straggling sailors finding a way across the rugged ice was the 524 foot oreboat J.H. BARTOW, of E.D. Carter's Erie Steamship Company. From the BAR-

TOW's texas deck her master, Captain White, had been watching the AURANIA's plight just as his counterparts on the PEAVEY and WELLS. And just like the others the BARTOW was stuck firmly in the ice and all he could do was watch through his binoculars. Shortly it became evident to Captain White that the group was headed for his boat. This made sense, considering that he was about a half mile closer to the sinking AURANIA than the other boats. Through his binoculars Captain White saw the approaching men having a rough go over the ice. In some places the surface was honeycombed and legs would occasionally crunch through past the knee. Plenty of luck would have to come into play if they were to make the BARTOW.

Captain Pringle's refugees had struggled for two and a half hours before reaching the BARTOW. As they approached, Captain White had ladders put over the side and the lifeboats swung out and lowered to the ice to help elevate the crew to the deck. In the galley the BARTOW's cook had extra coffee and hot soup prepared in large quantities for the AURANIA's crew arrival. While the sailors were boarding the BARTOW, a chorus of shouts rang from the steamer's rail and multiple fingers pointed in the direction of the AURANIA. Rolling on her beam, with her spars touching the ice, the red-hulled steamer went to the bottom at half past ten in the morning.

Finally managing to work free of the ice, the GEORGE W. PEAVEY arrived at the locks exactly nine hours after the AURANIA went down. Over the lock wall Captain Boyce shouted the narrative of the sunken Corrigan boat, and the news spread through the Soo almost as quickly as the smallpox rumor. Of course, the facts got fairly twisted. The red-hulled steamer crushed by the ice was reported as a downbounder, and the luckless crew were said to have staggered across ten miles of ice to get to safety. As the facts continued to inflate from mouth to ear, the PEAVEY passed through the locks and steamed passively down the St. Marys River. That same day some 44 lakeboats broke free of the bay and headed past Whitefish Point in a grand parade. The blockade was finally broken.

It took more than 42 hours from the time Captain Pringle's boat went under, until the BARTOW managed to free herself from Whitefish Bay's frigid grip and bring him and his crew to the Canadian Soo. At five o'clock in the morning on the first day of May, 1909 the AURANIA's crew was unloaded thankfully from their rescue steamer. By chartered tug, the bunch were transported across the river to the American side and gathered at the Murray Hill Hotel for breakfast. Captain Pringle did not waste an expletive in his effort to berate the masters of the two Peavey boats for

Cut down by spring ice on Whitefish Bay, the AURANIA sleeps forever, buried in the mud up to her water line and cradled in a trench 430 feet below the surface.

Author's Concept

not coming to his rescue. Little time was left for any counter points of view as the whole group boarded a Cleveland-bound train and headed back to Corrigan territory. With their departure from the Soo, the loss of the AURANIA, like the winter ice, simply melted away.

For the decades that followed the AURANIA's sinking, and forever more, the oreboats will crush across the frozen surface of Whitefish Bay to open the season, never giving a thought to the many wrecks that rest below the ice. One in particular, sitting on the bottom of the bay just off the steamer track, happens to be Captain Pringle's command, the AURANIA. In 1989, however, an expedition from the Great Lakes Shipwreck Historical Society, led by research diver Tom Farnquist, paid a visit to the ice water museum's AURANIA gallery. Hovering over the grave site aboard the research vessel GRAYLING, a remote submersible camera was lowered and the boat was found in a trench 430 feet deep, a mile and a half off Isle Parisienne, her deck a jumble of cables, lines and debris. Squatting upright in the mud up to her waterline, the AURANIA will wait preserved in the darkness for all time. Too deep for divers to reach and too obscure for boat watchers or lake mariners to remember, she is truly a forgotten exhibit.

Exactly why the AURANIA suddenly sprang a leak and went to the bottom will doubtless never be known, but the cause is likely to be a combination of her touching Iroquois Point and taking an already tender hull in to buck heavy ice. The cause matters little now, as the big boats shove past the forgotten AURANIA, fighting the spring ice to open each season. There is ore, grain and coal to bring down and little time to think about the boats that had lost their battles with the seasonal ice and now rest deep below in the silent blackness. These are simply the rites of spring at Sault Saint Marie—and around the Great Lakes.

Along Pridgeon's Line

Another wave of glacial water slapped Reuben Burns directly in the ear and broke solidly over his head. A second or two later the wave was spent and Burns felt himself sliding down the backside of the swell. When his ears cleared he could once again hear the wind roaring past. It was the first hours of Friday September 10th, 1875, and Lake Michigan wanted to swallow him whole . . . of that he was sure. With his elbows and knees he tried to get a better grip on the piece of wreckage that was now his life raft. Again he felt himself quickly raised up the side of another wave. Tucking his chin to his chest, he held his breath as the whitecap slapped him once more. His hands were too numb for him to know if he still had a good grip on the shattered pilothouse that was keeping him afloat. It seemed as if the waves would never stop coming—until finally one overwhelmed him. The night was so dark that he could not distinguish the sky from the seas. His sole companion in this suffering was the boat's second cook, adrift and semiconscious on the same wreckage. It probably would have been of little comfort had Burns known they were far from alone in this plight, for nearby were the drifting survivors of another shattered laker and soon there would be the crew of a third boat.

As the bright orange sun pushed over the horizon it brought no hint of warmth, only light; light that revealed the second cook's lifeless form as it slipped from the makeshift raft and vanished into what remained of the waves. Burns knew that before long it would be his body drifting away. Overhead the sky had turned bright blue with puffy cold clouds rushing past. The wind still whistled with a vengeance, and the lake was a green-gray color that occasionally reflected the blue sky. Summoning the strength to lift his head, Burns looked around the cantankerous horizon. He had no way of knowing that he was floating, powerless, right in the middle of Lake Michigan, over 20 miles from land.

Through the bitter day Reuben Burns drifted atop his wreckage raft. As he saw the sun sinking toward the west, he felt his strength sinking as well. Soon would be the dark and the air would get colder. He knew all too well that in the night the lake would digest him and leave not a trace. Like an open-handed insult it continued to slap him, one wave after another. Through the day several schooners had passed in the distance, each one draining a

Like many similar boats of her era, the EQUINOX and her near-twin MENDOTA sailed the lakes, carrying passengers and anything that would fit in her hold.

little of his hope with it. There was no reason to believe that the coming night would be any different.

Downbound for Chicago, plowing through Lake Michigan's chop came the schooner HAVANA. The 306 ton, 135 foot schooner had the wind at her heels and was making good time down the lake. Shortly before seven o'clock in the evening, those aboard the HAVANA spotted something bobbing in the waves, large and white and from a distance no regular shape. Striking her sails, Captain Hugh Ross had the schooner slowed and drew near the object. Floating ahead was what seemed to be the remains of a steamer's pilothouse, and clinging to it there appeared to be the body of a dead crewman. With pikepoles at the ready the schooner's crew prepared to recover the floater, but as they drew close, the body suddenly stirred and came to life with a feeble wave. In short order the refugee was pulled over the rail, but the lake had left him semiconscious, so the HAVANA's crew quickly carried him to the shelter of the schooner's fo'c'sle. It would be awhile before he could mutter more than his name and that of his vessel, the EQUINOX.

Unknown to those aboard the HAVANA, another schooner bearing a different piece of the EQUINOX's puzzle, had been picked up by the tug PROTECTION off Chicago and brought into the harbor. As the schooner EMMA A. MAYES nudged up to the pier, her master Captain Edward Lusk wasted no time in telling the story of the MAYES and her towing steamer EQUINOX. The MAYES herself was in rough shape. Heeled over in a bad list, with her cargo shifted, the schooner was sporting a badly split foresail. It was evident that only through the skill of her crew had the windgrabber managed to come off the lake.

A week before the EMMA A. MAYES turned up in Chicago, the story of the EQUINOX started, far up the twisting murk of the Saginaw River at an East Saginaw dock. There the slow process of loading a cargo of 5,130 barrels of salt consigned to Chicago was proceeding. Constructed in 1857 at Buffalo, New York, by Frederick Nelson Jones, the EQUINOX was a typical Great Lakes propeller of the day. Sliding off the builder's ways at the Ohio Street shipyard between Chicago and Wabash streets, her sleek wooden hull had all of the characteristics of a true monster. From her stern rail along her graceful curving deck to the peak of her high bluff bow, she measured 187 feet, 620 tons burden, with a steam powerplant that could produce 448 horsepower. Across her deck she spanned 31 feet between the tall hogging arches. Passenger accommodations were affixed to the main deck and atop it a multi-sided pilothouse. Below these fixtures was an enclosed cargo deck that was accessible through sideport gangways. She could carry almost any cargo below decks, from barreled flour to teams of horses. The whole profile was crowned aft with a tall smoke-stack and forward with a single towering mast.

Enrolled into service at the Buffalo Creek District on May 12th, 1857 the propeller EQUINOX was owned by the Dean Richmond concerns. In 1865, these same operators had a "tween-decks" added to her hold, probably to better facilitate the carrying of barreled cargo. As of September 13th, 1865 her new tonnage was 870.51, consistent with such a modification. Dean Richmond sold the EQUINOX in May of 1867. That year she began running for the Union Steamboat Company between Buffalo and Chicago. This was a route that would become the regular path for most of the boat's career.

By that summer-like Sunday along the Saginaw waterfront in 1875, the EQUINOX was owned by the Cleveland partnership Garrison and Scott, the latter being the boat's Master, Captain Dwight Scott. In the background of the vessel's management were two silent partners, W.H. Sullivan and Captain John Pridgeon, both of Detroit. Captain Pridgeon was one of the most prominent vessel barons around the Great Lakes and managed to hold interest in a large fleet of lakeboats. Many of his lakers ran between Sarnia, Ontario and Chicago. So dominating was his influence along this passage that in marine circles the route had been dubbed "Pridgeon's Line," implying that the stretch of water up Lake Huron, through the Straits of Mackinaw and down to Chicago was owned by the captain and his fleet.

The EQUINOX had spent her fair share running along Pridgeon's Line, but the most recent contract had brought her to Saginaw. In 18 seasons of service the big wooden steamer had worked hard and the stresses of her toil were beginning to show. One fact was that the insurance rating of the once elegant steamer had slipped to B1. This was not surprising, considering her advancing age. In tow of the EQUINOX this trip would be the schooner EMMA A. MAYES, Captain Lusk's command. This would be only the second trip for the EQUINOX with the MAYES as consort. For an extended period of time the steamer had been paired with the 139 foot schooner GUIDING STAR, but the officers of the two boats had apparently had some kind of falling out and the partnering of the two had been terminated. Surely what consort was attached to her stern mattered little to the EQUINOX, for she seemed more than prepared to hiss her way once more along Pridgeon's Line.

Supervising the loading of Captain Scott's EQUINOX as she took the last barrels of salt was First Mate Cyrus Woodruff, who was a captain in his own right. Formerly the master of the MILTON D. WARD, Mate Woodruff had been caught up in the ebb and flow of Great Lakes commerce and found himself earning his living as the number two man aboard the EQUINOX. Even in modern times it is not unusual for a certified master of vessels to work on occasion as mate. In fact, this practice has become almost a tradition on the lakes.

Also aboard the EQUINOX were two special passengers, on a late season sabbatical. From the shelter of the Sacred Heart convent in Detroit, Captain Scott's 19-year-old daughter Minnie had come to visit her father and to experience the adventure of the wild lakes. Accompanying her was the captain's 17-year-old granddaughter, Hattie. For Captain Scott, whose spouse had passed away several years before, the company of the two maidens was an incredible treat. The business of the EQUINOX kept him away from these "apples of his eye," for nearly eight months of each year, and they were his only family. When a person is away like that, time passes swiftly . . . friends who are seen just during the winter months, and relatives who are spoken to only at holidays appear to age unexpectedly. Likewise, children grow up at a breathtaking rate, seeming almost to be a different person each time they are encountered. Naturally, Captain Scott was delighted to have the young ladies aboard and made sure they were shown all of the boat's best courtesy. Obviously the atmosphere about the EQUINOX was light-hearted, and relaxed. These were the days when some of the non-licensed crew were simple drifters with a taste for demon rum, and captains were virtual tyrants—when "the old man" is happy, the crew is cheerful.

There is an old superstition that says nothing good can come from a voyage that is started on a Sunday. Of course every time something goes afoul with some luckless laker, those who subscribe to such legend search for her day of departure to fulfill the fable. With no regard for the Sunday fallacy, the jovial EQUINOX steamed from the Saginaw dock with the schooner EMMA A. MAYES dutifully in tow astern, on Sunday September 5th, 1875. Early

Monday found the two boats creeping up the widening expanse of Saginaw Bay. The weather Lake Huron was presenting was a breath of summer belated, and up in the EQUINOX's pilothouse, Mate Woodruff had the majority of the boat's windows lowered, allowing the freshwater breeze to drift through. Flanking the mate and enjoying the fine day was the boat's wheelsman Reuben Burns. This was the way to start a trip to Chicago!

All around the EQUINOX, cabin windows and doors were propped open, and those not hard at work with the daily chores found good reason go out on deck. Along the cargo deck the top half of a number of the gangways was opened to the breeze, and strung up at the boat's promenade a small load of laundry waved toward the EMMA A. MAYES. From the schooner, Captain Lusk kept a casual eye on the steamer as it churned ahead in the sticky haze. If it were not for the lake's cool breath, the day might even have been considered uncomfortable. As darkness closed in Monday evening, the EQUINOX and consort were coming abeam Sturgeon Point, their lights illuminating the cabin windows as a row of amber squares. From shore, that was the image that marked the passing lakers, a simple row of amber lights floating like a ghost across the lake's distance. Everyone aboard the two boats held out the hope that the current weather conditions would prevail all along the 500 odd miles of Pridgeon's line that stretched to Chicago.

By Tuesday afternoon it appeared that summer was about to expire, for the west the sky had become unfriendly and dark gray, swallowing the sun long before it hit the horizon. From the rail of the MAYES, Captain Lusk gazed toward the blackening distance. His instincts told him that the dark curtain to the west predictably marked the last act of the summer's fair weather festival. Since there was no form of weather reporting or forecasting available to the

EQUINOX and MAYES, no one aboard the boats had any way of knowing that line of dark clouds marked the leading squall of a powerful and fast-moving cold front trailing more than 250 miles to the west. Behind the front, a strong northeast flow of air built gale-force winds—the whole nightmare was headed directly for Lake Michigan.

By 4 p.m., a sinister quiet had fallen upon the pair of lakers, and from the EMMA A. MAYES it was easy to hear the voices of those on the EQUINOX, as well as the clanks and hisses of the work aboard her, echoing across the water. The sky now appeared divided in half, and Captain Lusk could clearly see the flashes of lightning followed by long-delayed thunder. In anticipation of the coming weather, the schooner's master had put her crew to work securing the boat for rough weather. As they worked, the time span between the flashes of lightning and the thunder shortened, for the storm was charging closer. This merely added to the urgency of the crew's work as they attempted to ready the boat. Swiftly the winds began to freshen, and moments later the rain came in whipping sheets. The precipitation strafed horizontally ahead of the shrieking wind, and the seas came up instantly, having built over the 50 plus miles between the Wisconsin shore and the two boats. The waves quickly set the pair of lakers on their beam ends with a continual rolling action. Surely, this was a powerful system, out to test every vessel in its path.

Unknown to those aboard EQUINOX and MAYES, another team of lakers was being set upon by the squall just a few scant miles behind. When approaching Mackinaw, the steamer MENDOTA and a two-barge tow found themselves assaulted by the southwest storm. To say that the EQUINOX and MENDOTA were two of a kind would not be correct, but to say that they were of the same class of vessel would be much closer. Constructed at Cleveland just three months after the EQUINOX entered service, the MENDOTA was of 785 tons burden and basically outfitted the same. Equipped with sideports to her cargo deck as well as passenger accommodations on top, the steamer was of screw propulsion and able to pull a string of loaded schooners. Upon her enrollment the MENDOTA went straight to work for up-start vesselman William Crosthwaite.

In command of the MENDOTA on this rough 1875 autumn passage was Captain A.S. Fairbanks, and behind the steamer were the schooner-barges MORNING STAR and EVENING STAR. All three boats were loaded with coal at Buffalo and hauling for Chicago along Pridgeon's Line. Onboard for this trip was a special guest, William S. Crosthwaite, the 21 year old son of the MENDOTA's owner. Unlike the guests aboard the EQUINOX, young Crosthwaite was a bit reluctant to be aboard the MENDOTA. He felt deep down that somehow the family maritime business was not his true calling. The pressures for a son to follow in his father's footsteps were far greater in the starched collar days of the 1870s than they are today, so William Jr. found himself aboard the MENDOTA, reluctantly, to learn the business.

Shortly after the squall struck the MENDOTA and her consorts, Captain Fairbanks decided that he did not like the dusting that his boat was being exposed to and elected to run for shelter. Turning just a couple of points to the south, he ducked the trio behind a point which would afford lee from a southwest wind. Before the boats reached that shelter, the squall passed and the winds died from a shriek to a bluster. With winds continuing from the southwest, Captain Fairbanks elected to put in after passing the Straits of Mackinac, knowing that such a wind would build waves the full length of Lake Michigan. In such a sea the captain did not want to find himself, so the MENDOTA would lay at the Kelderhouse dock until the lake simmered down.

At two o'clock Thursday afternoon the MENDOTA and her barges set out once again down Lake Michigan. Shortly after the three boats had rolled onto the open lake, the winds began to shift rapidly to the northwest and blow a gale. All the boats were taking quite a beating from the following sea that had developed ahead of the winds, so again Captain Fairbanks turned the MENDOTA. This time his maneuver was an effort to run against the seas toward the shelter of South Manitou Island. Ironically, as the MENDOTA was turning, her cousin vessel, the EQUINOX, was passing her downbound and unnoticed in the dark distance. After pounding head to the wind for some time, Captain Fairbanks determined that the trio was making no headway and turned yet another time to flee before the wind.

Both the MENDOTA and EQUINOX were headed toward Chicago with a full gale at their heels, the EQUINOX nearly four hours in the lead. Both boats were almost two full days tardy in moving down the lake. While a written record of the movements of Captain Fairbanks's boat exists, there are none from Captain Scott's EQUINOX. Considering that the two boats were delayed by nearly the exact same interval, it is safe to reason that Captain Scott's actions in avoiding the storm were similar to those of Captain Fairbanks with the MENDOTA. It mattered little, as now both boats were deeply into Lake Michigan's grip.

On the schooner EMMA A. MAYES, Captain Lusk, like his counterpart Captain Scott aboard the towing steamer EQUINOX, had prepared for a storm, but expected nothing close to what Lake Michigan was delivering. The ripping wind instantly found the schooner's stowed canvas and began to unwrap it from her booms. Rolling to her gunwhales, the MAYES was shipping water and in danger of being overwhelmed. All hands of the storm-tossed schooner took to the deck and rigging in an attempt to save their boat. As the crew of the EMMA A. MAYES struggled with her rigging, sudden shouts from the EQUINOX drew their attention. Bounding his way to the rolling schooner's bow, Captain Lusk tried to distinguish what was being shouted from the steamer. He thought he recognized the voice as that of Mate Woodruff, and over the roaring of the wind it sounded as if he was calling "cast off your line, cast off your line," but it was difficult to understand.

It was clear that there was something radically wrong with the steamer EQUINOX, but the captain of the MAYES had his hands full saving his own boat. He had only time enough to release the line and then tend to the well-being of the schooner. As the line was let go, the screams of a female voice split the storm. "We're drowning! we're drowning!" the cries seemed to say. And with that, those aboard the MAYES watched in horror as the big steamer dipped, rolled onto her stern quarter and with a roar was swallowed by the lake—leaving nothing but a hole in the water. Left peering through the darkness, the crew of the MAYES was in complete shock. The idea that a 187 foot lakeboat could plunge to the bottom in a matter of seconds was utterly unimaginable, but the fact remained—there was only the lake where the EQUINOX had been moments before.

Alone in the storm, the crew of the MAYES now had to collect their wits, and began to run with the winds. It was two o'clock Friday morning. With what sails could be mustered, the schooner began pounding toward Chicago—there was no chance of searching for survivors in the pitch black night. The winds had now turned and were blowing out of the north, northeast, the waves had become mountainous and the temperature was beginning to plummet as Captain Lusk nursed his charge down the lake, unknowingly leaving Wheelsman Burns and the luckless second cook adrift on the EQUINOX's broken pilothouse.

Nearly in the wake of the sunken EQUINOX came the MENDOTA and her barges, without an inkling of the disaster that had occurred ahead. Captain Fairbanks, in fact, had the survival of his own boat foremost on his mind. Starting around midnight the MENDOTA had begun to take water through her gangways, and by the time the unfortunate EQUINOX was plunging to her doom, all of the MENDOTA's crew were manning their boat's pumps. It is certain that young Mr. Crosthwaite's feelings of reluctance were turning to terror, as he watched the best efforts of the steamer's men thwarted by the incoming lake. In utter astonishment, he saw waves bigger than he could ever imagine crash over the promenade deck and wash the full length of the big wooden steamer. The size of the MENDOTA and the feel of her thick wooden timbers had always impressed William, and each time he saw her or walked aboard along her gangplank, he'd thought what a monstrous machine she was. Now she was like a rowboat among the waves and no match for Lake Michigan's fury.

About three o'clock came a resounding bang as the towing hawser to the MENDOTA's barges parted and the schooners were set adrift in the maelstrom. Immediately the MORNING STAR, which had been first in the tow, released the EVENING STAR, to give both boats more maneuverability. This complicated matters for Captain James Bennett of the EVENING STAR, as his boat was already in a leaking condition and he needed all hands at the two pumps. The pumping operation would have to be halted so crew could man the sails. Meanwhile, from the MENDOTA, the lights of the two schooners seemed to vanish in the darkness.

At dawn Friday morning, both barges were clearly visible from the MENDOTA and appeared to have sails up and be making good weather of it, but the steamer was in a far different condition. Her fires out and the water nearly up to her deck, it was just a matter of time before she would go. An emergency sail had been raised after her steam went down—it was promptly blown to rags by the wind. When all hope was given up, the crew was ordered to put on life vests and prepare the lifeboats. Captain Scott's wife and father, who had been aboard for a pleasure trip, were each given two life belts, as if to insure their security. The captain, mate, first engineer, two wheelsmen, two deck hands and William Crosthwaite launched one of the steamer's two lifeboats and were preparing to get away, when Crosthwaite spotted Mrs. Scott and the captain's father huddled near the pilothouse. Apparently, in the confusion, Captain Scott had thought them to be in the other lifeboat. As the crowded yawl was lowering into the rolling seas, Crosthwaite leaped back onto the MENDOTA's cabin and struggled to the rescue of the two guests. When he reached the Scotts, the ship's cook was there as well, and the whole bunch began to struggle toward the yawl, which Captain Scott was maneuvering back toward them. At that instant the MENDOTA sank like a stone beneath them—shattering the deck houses and pulling the lifeboats and all aboard into a giant swirling vortex.

When William S. Crosthwaite surfaced he was surrounded by heaving wreckage and struggling survivors. The yawl had been overturned and was carried off by the wind, so those lucky enough to surface alive began to cling to whatever pieces of the MENDOTA would keep them afloat. Crosthwaite, along with second engineer Ed Hughes, managed to crawl aboard a large chunk of the boat's crushed cabin and dragged the semi-conscious cook with them. In the distance they could see some of the MENDOTA's other people struggling to gather makeshift rafts. Now there were two groups of castaways drifting upon the remains of two different lakeboats within a few scant miles of one another. But Lake Michigan was not yet satisfied and set her ire toward yet another boat and crew.

With her sails finally set, the schooner-barge EVENING STAR had her crew hard at work on the pumps. By 11 o'clock Friday morning, Captain Bennett saw clearly that their efforts were useless, as some seven feet of lake water was filling her hold, and she no longer answered to the helm. It was time to surrender the EVENING STAR to the lake and hope that the sacrifice would be enough to persuade the lake to spare the souls aboard. The order given, all seven of the schooner's crew jammed into the 15 foot yawl and abandoned the EVENING STAR. As the water sloshed aboard, the crew bailed for their lives . . . and drifted before the storm . . . there were three sets of castaways on the surface of Lake Michigan.

By daylight Friday the EQUINOX's surviving consort EMMA A. MAYES was in sight of land and by eight o'clock that same morning dropped her hooks just outside the port of Chicago. As a matter of routine, the tug PROTECTION observed the schooner rocking at anchor and made a bee line out to claim her rightful towing charter. Safely in port, Captain Lusk and those of his crew spent the day telling of the tragic loss of the EQUINOX. Through that nasty Saturday the telegraphs clicked with reports of chaos across the lakes, and by evening the compilation gave insight to the rude storm. The listings were incomplete as there was no mention of the MENDOTA or her barges.

Having spent 27 hours adrift, constantly bailing, the crew of the EVENING STAR finally felt the stones and sand of the beach grind beneath the yawl boat. It was just after two o'clock Saturday afternoon when they dragged the boat clear of the lake near the town of Amsterdam and began to pace around and rub their limbs in an effort to cure the numbness. Captain Bennett had lost his boat, but apparently that was enough to satisfy the lake, at least in his case.

On Monday, two full days after the EQUINOX went to the bottom, the schooner HAVANA was towed into Chicago harbor. Onboard was Wheelsman Reuben Burns, now fully recovered from his odyssey on the shattered pilothouse. Shortly after the HAVANA's arrival, word spread along the waterfront that there was a survivor of the EQUINOX when all aboard were thought lost. In quest of answers to the steamer's disaster, the curious as well as the professionals headed for the waterfront. Chief among them was Captain Lusk and the crew of the EMMA A. MAYES. A crowd gathered at the HAVANA as Reuben Burns, flanked by Captain Ross, told his story. Those gathered around stood with wide eyes and intent ears as the sole survivor recalled the EQUINOX's last moments. Shortly after the storm hit the steamer and her consort, the EQUINOX began to roll heavily in the seas. Reuben Burns was at his post in the pilothouse with Captain Scott when the storm peaked, and no sooner had the EQUINOX settled into her normal heavy weather posture, than the steamer sprung a leak on the port side aft. The leak was of massive proportions and it was all too clear that the EQUINOX was being overwhelmed. Captain Scott sent the mate aft to call to the MAYES and try to get her to "come along side" a shout that in the storm could easily be garbled to "cast off your line." Crowding on the fantail were most of the passengers and crew, but some of the crew took after the port lifeboat. That side of the boat was down the lowest, and eleven men entered the boat and started lowering. Sensing that the boat was beginning to slip, Burns and Captain Scott abandoned the pilothouse and dashed aft toward the starboard lifeboat. Their scramble was far too late, for the EQUINOX heeled over on top of the port lifeboat and its occupants.

The steamer sank beneath the running feet of the captain and wheelsman, with the captain catching the gangway and being pulled down. Burns and the second cook were lucky enough to pop up near the wreckage of the pilot-house, and Burns was lucky enough to be seen by the HAVANA.

Late on Monday the bark NAIAD sailed into Manitowoc, Wisconsin and aboard were five survivors with a story of their own. Greeting dry land across the sailing vessel's gangplank, came what remained of the MENDOTA's people, First Mate J. Carney, First Engineer Amos Ness, Second Engineer Ed Hughes and his raft companion William S. Crosthwaite. Last of all came a heartbroken Captain Fairbanks who had lost his wife, father and command to the lake in one bitter stroke. If an emptied soul existed anywhere on the lakes that day, it was his. All of the castaways were picked up Sunday evening when the NAIAD had stumbled onto the flotsam of the poor MENDOTA. What few persons the lake had spared were all now on dry land . . . the others would remain forever on Lake Michigan.

In the weeks that followed the storm, there were investigations and summonses filed by the steamboat inspectors John P. Farrer and John B. Warren of the district of Chicago. All of this was overshadowed by the mystery that was evolving over the whereabouts of Reuben Burns, who although quite willing to talk about the EQUINOX's wreck when he came off the rescue schooner, had now vanished. There was great speculation that he had been spirited into hiding, to sell his information to the inspectors, or to bleed the insurance companies who had underwritten the EQUINOX. In later days there appeared the following article in the Chicago Inter Ocean: *"Private and special dispatches from Port Huron say a man has shipped on the propeller ST. JOSEPH, who gives his name as Burns or Barr,*

Down to her rails, the MENDOTA sinks while her barges fend for themselves.

Author's Concept

and who claims to be the sole survivor of the propeller EQUINOX, 'but wants it kept quiet.' No publicity will be given to the fact, as a matter of course, because that's what newspapers are for. Steamboat inspectors please take notice." That simple paragraph, like others, was meant to stir up as much mystery as possible. The fact was that the news reporting of the day was nearly as twisted as it is in modern times. Wheelsman Burns had his name misreported as Barr, and Burr. There were even dramatic accounts of the sinkings, that had young Crosthwaite leaping aboard a sinking vessel to save his panicked wife, and the two of them drowning in each other's arms. Crosthwaite was not married and the whole news item had been concocted—but it was picked up and printed by the Associated Press as fact. Over time, Burns, like the EQUINOX, got his wish and faded into obscurity.

Young William S. Crosthwaite, in years to follow, found his true calling as a minister. What 1870s family could argue with such a calling? Surely the senior Mr. Crosthwaite could not. William Jr.'s calling took him to the wild West, across the Great Plains and into the American desert. Perhaps he felt a real need for a man of his calling in the West, or perhaps the horror of Lake Michigan's frigid temper compelled him to travel as far from the freshwater seas as he could get.

In all, the EQUINOX took 25 people to the bottom with her, and the MENDOTA took 12 just four hours later, in virtually the same spot. More than a century ago and as of this writing they rest there, about eight miles off the Sable Points. It is a part of Lake Michigan where the bottom dips as low as several hundred feet and in places rises to less than 80 feet in depth. Literally hundreds of wrecks are scattered over this region and among them, undiscovered, are the EQUINOX and MENDOTA. Since 1875 they have been the obscure and unmarked grave of more than three dozen souls. On fair summer days, research divers in small boats armed with sidescan sonar, trace the bottom in quest of long-forgotten lakeboats. Year after year they act out this lonely, cold, damp obsession in the hope of casting a ray of light on the lost commands, homes and lives of the ones who made their careers on the lakes so long ago. Possibly this summer as these electronic explorers crisscross Lake Michigan, the pen will graph the image of a small wooden hulk—and at last mark the grave of the EQUINOX or the MENDOTA. They are the sole monuments remaining of the people and vessels that once worked along Pridgeon's Line.

Among the Jumble of King Lumber

In the early 1880s there was great confusion in the Great Lakes shipping industry. Not only did vessels scamper about like mice in an abandoned warehouse, but there were cases in which some boats carried the same name as other lakers. At one point there were three boats wearing the name MAYFLOWER—a tug, a schooner, and a steamer—and many lakeboats named ANTELOPE. Over the years preceding the turn of the century 13 boats, from tugs to schooners to steamers, had ANTELOPE painted on their bow. To complicate matters, these boats seemed to move about beyond the marine column's ability to report on them.

During the 1881 season, the propeller ANTELOPE and the schooner-barge of the same name had been playing leap-frog in and out of the Saginaw River. On Monday, September 12, it was the wooden steamer's turn in the river, and Captain Bule was guiding from the ANTELOPE's pilothouse. As the steam-barge's propeller churned the murky waters of the river, the schooner-barge COMMODORE came in tow behind her. Both boats were in from a lumber run to Tonawanda, New York and were returning empty to pick up another load. Lumber from the mills along the Saginaw River would be stacked aboard the boats and hauled to Buffalo, Tonawanda or other points east. After unloading, the return trip normally would be made with coal aboard. It was a glamorless, common toil that the ANTELOPE performed regularly for Bay City's Curtis and Lindsay shipping company. Dull as the routine might be, Captain Bule and the ANTELOPE's crew knew all too well that over the last four years their little boat had been through more than her fair share of scrapes. From snags to bumps and groundings, the steamer was forced to undergo some 14,000 dollars in repairs. This staggering sum, by 1881 standards, was near half the cost of a new boat. Without doubt Captain Bule wanted no further entanglements.

Constructed at Newport, Michigan, in 1861, the ANTELOPE was one of many in her class to taste freshwater, an elegant combination passenger and cargo steamer with a pair of high arches gracing her beams, and sideports for cargo. Sliding from the ways at John L. Wolverton's yard, the wooden steamer's hull measured 186 feet in length, 31 feet in beam and a modest 11 feet in depth, with a burden of 600 tons. Her initial enrollment came in Detroit on August 17th of the year of her construction. She was assigned the official number of 571 and went immediately to work along the Buffalo to Chicago run. By 1866 the town of Newport had been re-christened Marine City, and the fruit of its boatyard, the ANTELOPE, was being lengthened to 201 feet, bringing her tonnage up to 797 gross tons. At the same time an additional foot was added to her depth. With her new enhanced capacity, the ANTELOPE went back to work looking forward to a prosperous career.

As the 1867 season was drawing to a close, the ANTELOPE was squatting at the feet of Reed's Elevator in Buffalo, New York, unloading a cargo of barreled flour and bulk wheat. There were 600 casks of flour and 1,700 bushels of grain yet to be unloaded when fire erupted near the boat's boilers and spread so rapidly that the engine crew was quickly forced from their stations. Fast thinking on the part of the ANTELOPE's engineer and officers resulted in the scuttling of the burning boat, but this was not before the flames had consumed her to the water's edge. When the ice cleared the following spring, the sad remains of the ANTELOPE were raised and towed to Clark's Dry Dock of Detroit, where she was rebuilt, and returned to service on the 10th of May, 1869. Now she came out with a gross tonnage of 915, a significant increase over her pre-fire burden. Although there are no records to prove it, this likely represents the addition of a second deck for the handling of packaged or barreled cargo. She was rebuilt again just six years later, changing her tonnage to 750 gross, and again there is no specific record, but this change would be consistent with the removal of an extra deck and most of her passenger accommodations, to better facilitate the hauling of lumber. This was the somewhat worn laker that Captain Bule worked on the Saginaw River. She was nothing special, just a working boat on a busy waterway.

Easing up to the McGraw dock, the two lumberboats put lines ashore and gangplanks were plopped upon the rails and gangways. At dockside a gang of stevedores, or "dock wollopers," were poised for the job of loading the ANTELOPE and COMMODORE.

The loading and unloading of lumber was a time-consuming process largely done by hand, as one after another, the wollopers would stomp up the ramps, carrying the cargo board by board. Sometimes as many as 50 or 60 laborers would work the stacks of wood. A full day could be taken up in the loading of lumber one plank at a time and so it was with the ANTELOPE and COMMODORE.

By Wednesday the calloused hands of the stevedores had neatly stacked over 300,000 board feet aboard the ANTELOPE and 775,000 aboard the COMMODORE, and the two boats joined the river's jumble of tugs, schooners, barges and steamers in the movement of "king lumber." That same day the total product moved by the fleet from the Saginaw River totalled 3,627,000 board feet. The sailings of the lakers unfortunately were overshadowed by the boasting of the captain of the tug WITCH, who had just run up the river, towing the barge G.H. WAUD. "We just run from Bay City to Crow Island in only one hour," he bragged to those shore-side, "and then come back in the same time with that barge HUNGERFORD! Who's next for the fastest tug on the river?" The people standing about the dock listened to every detail of the tug's feat, as the ANTELOPE and her barge slipped meekly past. You see, the shipping of more than three and a half million feet of lumber was considered a slow day along the Saginaw River in 1881.

During the next three days, the two boats traversed the freshwater seas toward Tonawanda. There the COMMODORE was dropped at the Hathaway dock to unload and the ANTELOPE went to the Export Lumber Company to do the same. Once again, the parade of dock wollopers marched along the gangplanks to unload the boats one plank at a time. Finished, the two boats set out toward Buffalo to pick up coal and start back for Bay City. While in Buffalo, Captain Bule secured a deal to tow the barges GOULD and PECK back as well as the COMMODORE. The GOULD and PECK already were topped off with coal, and had been waiting for a steamer to pull them up the lakes.

As the ANTELOPE swung clear of the Buffalo harbor, a fair bit of September wind was ripping the length of Lake Erie. Turning onto a 249 degree course, Captain Bule checked the steamer's tow of three barges, which seemed to be riding well. It was just after eight o'clock Friday evening September 23rd, and those who made their livelihood working the lakes were getting a familiar taste of autumn's temper. From the ANTELOPE's pilothouse, Captain Bule determined the winds to be just a bothersome bluster and pointed the steamer directly into the developing chop.

On her present course, the little lakeboat would hiss 59 miles before passing 3 miles abeam Long Point at four a.m. After that, it was 134 miles of open, irritated Lake Erie until reaching the Southeast Shoal and Point Pelee just before 10 o'clock Saturday night. The graveyard gap between the point and Pelee Island would be the most treacherous part of the trip, but then, Pelee Passage is always a threat to moving in and out of Lake Erie. A gap of only eight plus miles, the passage is lined with wadeable shoals, so a zigzag from the ANTELOPE's present 249 degree course to 290 on the compass would be required. That would be held for 55 minutes, then the steamer and consorts must swing nearly due west on a 275 course and, as time expired, run for the Detroit River on a 295 degree course. If all went well, they should clear Lake Erie at five a.m. Sunday morning.

Talk onboard the ANTELOPE Friday evening into Saturday, centered around the recent death of President John Garfield. Most of the port facilities on the American side were to close at mid-day Saturday and remain closed through Sunday, in a show of respect for the late President. This would be of little consequence to the ANTELOPE, as she would be simply sailing past Detroit on Sunday and did not plan to make port until late Monday night. Without regard to the time table, the passing of the nation's leader made for welcome conversation through the gray and stormy Saturday.

Darkness brought with it a fresh wind from the west southwest. What had been a depressing fall drizzle now turned into a whipping rain, and the ANTELOPE began to take a slight corkscrew in the increasing seas. By nine, the wind was blowing a gale and Captain Bule was having a bit of a time holding the boat against it. Spray was coming across the heaped deck cargo of the schooner-barges, and streams of water stained black with coal dust were running along the doorjambs and cracks. Peering through the rain-beaded pilothouse windows, the steamer's captain was beginning to feel that old tingle behind his ears. It appeared he was going to have to pull his tail across the passage through the pitch-black night in a heavy wind and rain—it was not going to be pleasant. As he ordered the first turn, the wind pounced on the ANTELOPE and grabbed her and her consorts with a fresh temper.

Around the other lakes the conditions had become equally appalling. A telegram from the Soo arrived at Detroit, reporting that a steam-barge thought to be the JARVIS LORN had slammed onto Isle Parisienne in Whitefish Bay. Storm winds bringing sheets of rain had driven the boat from her course and tossed her upon the island, just 10 miles short of the shelter at St. Marys River. From Marquette, a salvage crew had been dispatched to provide what aid might be needed.

Downbound through the St. Clair and Detroit rivers with a three barge tow, all lumber-laden, came the steamer MISSOURI. Unknown to her master, there had been a drilling and dredging operation at the Lime Kiln, but the crew and equipment had been laid off for the president's funeral. Behind, they had left a large pile of boulders, unmarked. Amidst the storm winds and blowing rain, the MISSOURI's bottom had no problem in finding the hidden obstruction. Striking with a series of jolts, the steamer at once began to leak. When the syphons were started, it became clear they easily would handle the seeping water, so the MISSOURI proceeded clear of the Detroit River and dropped her barges, then turned around and headed back to a friendly Detroit dry dock.

On the 290 degree course the ANTELOPE began to roll heavily. Looking behind, Captain Bule could see the dim amber lamps from his consorts, rolling out of sync with one another. Crazy seas began an assault on the steamer's beam, at times sending a solid spray over the deck. The wind screeched and howled as it ripped past the rigging. At the ANTELOPE's stern the towing hawser twisted and creaked as it pulled tight as a bar, with all she could muster, the little steam-barge hauled on her burden. It was a long 55 minutes, but the ANTELOPE cleared Pelee Passage (along with her barges) and headed for the Detroit River. The boat's master was relieved to bring the boats back into the wind. At 1:40 Sunday morning an exhausted Captain Bule and the master of each barge spotted the bright white light of Colchester Reef well off to his starboard bow. Apparently, he thought, he had been just a bit aggressive against the winds and had pulled a little to the south. No matter, he was in deep water and should easily be able to correct. Departing the 275 course, Captain Bule directed the wheelsman to turn a few points toward the north, to come closer to the Colchester Reef light. Just 20 minutes later the ANTELOPE jolted, throwing crew members to the deck.

For an instant, as Captain Bule struggled for footing, he thought that they had struck another vessel. Other than the ANTELOPE and her barges, however, there were no other vessels. As the captain regained his balance and the wheelsman steadied back at his post, there came a second jolt, then a third—and the ANTELOPE snagged to a halt. Everyone in the pilothouse now came to the agonizing realization of what had happened. The steamer had run aground at nearly full speed. The captain's immediate concern was that the barges would have the momentum to run up his stern. A quick look told him that they were not moving with anywhere near the forward way required to hit him. The gale-force wind was rapidly scrubbing off their seven plus miles per hour speed.

No sooner had the ANTELOPE come to a stop than the seas began to work her upon the rocks. Pushing his finger against the pilothouse window, her master erupted with disoriented anger, "There it is, there's the blasted Colchester light right there!" he roared. "We must be two miles south of the snags!" he shouted, slapping the back of his hand toward the opposite window. Captain Bule's rage was abruptly interrupted as the deck beneath his feet started to rotate counter-clockwise. From deep below, the hull gave a grinding moan. The winds had seized the barges, swinging them to the northeast. This action, combined with that of the seas, would break the steamer up if something were not done quickly. Wasting no time, Captain Bule ordered the towing hawser axed—and the COMMODORE, GOULD and PECK were set adrift. The ANTELOPE was alone on her perch.

A series of backing and turning maneuvers were attempted, but the ANTELOPE refused to move. Her snag was not so firm as to keep her from rocking about on the shoal with the cresting waves, it simply refused to let her go. Captain Bule felt his boat had been caught in a spider's web, and the more he worked to free her the more entrapped the steamer became. Continuous sharp seas smashed at the ANTELOPE's planking as she pounded on the submerged rocks. The seams began to open under the stress and water leaked aboard, mixing with the cargo. Only one desperate act could prevent the wooden laker from going to pieces on the reef—she would have to be scuttled.

Wet rust was hammered from the sea cocks as the engineer cracked them open, allowing gushers of Lake Erie to burst in. Ever so slowly, the steamer listed over and settled firmly onto the shoal. Sitting well over on her beam ends, the boat at least was relieved of the pounding that the seas had been inflicting. The only problem was that with the ship's bowels flooded, her fires were out and the crew would be forced to shelter in the tilted cabins, with no steam for the radiators. Through the night they waited, as the waves broke over their boat with a rumble like unending thunder.

Grudgingly dawn came and with it Captain Bule's realization that his boat had run smack onto Colchester Reef. But, if he was on the reef, where was the Colchester Reef lightship? And what of the light that everyone saw the night before? Scanning the near-by Canadian shore, it was easy to see that the light had been that of an anchored boat, north of the shoal. Unknown to Captain Bule, the Cambell Brothers Company, who had charge of the light, had opted to remove the Colchester Reef lightship . . . for whatever reasons. Now the ANTELOPE was heeled on the reef, the one reason they should have left well enough alone.

On Sunday, a small rescue armada from the Canada Wrecking Company set out to Colchester Reef and the stricken coal carriers. Steaming across the gray lake came the tug ERIE BELLE, to pick up the ANTELOPE's stray barges. With the BELLE came the tug JESSIE with the lightering schooner-barge ARGO in tow. Onboard the JESSIE, with his attention fixed out of the window, was Detroit wreck diver Frank Dwyer. Last came the tug PRINCE ALFRED carrying the manager of the wrecking company, Mr. McDonald. This whole fleet had set out from Amherstburg, Ontario and the entire operation was under the command of Captain Connolly of the JESSIE. Mr. McDonald was simply along to observe.

From the ANTELOPE's pilothouse Captain Bule saw the approaching rescue fleet, marked by billows of thick black coal smoke. At the same time, Captain Connolly and wreck diver Dwyer were looking back toward the stranded ANTELOPE. Dropping open the JESSIE's pilothouse window, Dwyer made an evaluation of the stranded steam-barge. "Looks like she's on there real good," he groaned

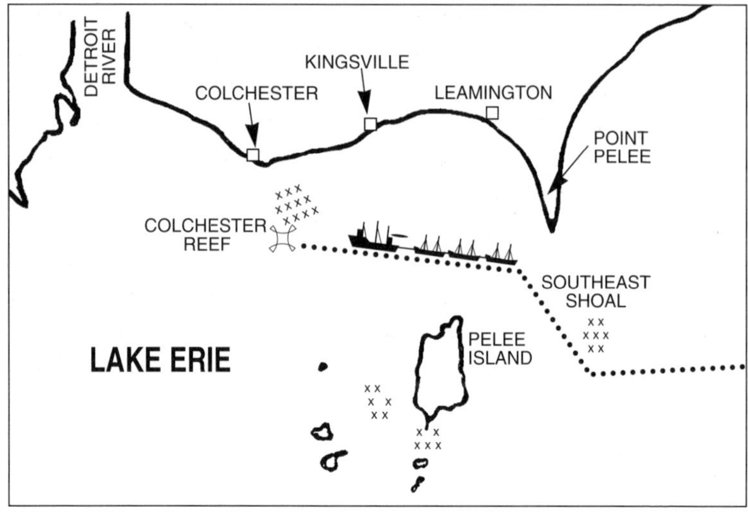

with a bit of a smile, "should make for a few days' work." Captain Connolly nodded in response. With the steamer heeled on the reef and her three barges anchored off in Pigeon Bay like three lost ducklings, it appeared the wreckers had their work cut out for them.

With the tug ERIE BELLE starting the task of gathering up the scattered barges, the PRINCE ALFRED and JESSIE took up positions on the ANTELOPE. In short order the ARGO was put on the steamer's beam, and the long process of lightering the ANTELOPE's coal cargo commenced. Huge wooden buckets were attached by block and tackle to the ARGO's masts and swung over the side, lowered to the stranded boat and filled by shovel. With a steam assist, the filled buckets were swung back to the ARGO and dumped aboard the schooner-barge—a laborious, back-breaking and most of all, time-consuming task. As soon as the ARGO was made fast to the ANTELOPE, the schooner's crew of laborers scrambled aboard and started shoveling. The concern now was that the weather might come up again before the ANTELOPE could be pulled free, and the wind and waves could smash the steamer like a raw egg. All those working on the luckless steamer kept in mind that on August 27th, almost exactly a month before the ANTELOPE went on, the tug MAY-FLOWER had been dashed to pieces in just that way on just that reef. There was a real sense of urgency hovering over Colchester Reef.

Sunday evening an anonymous tug unobtrusively sneaked the Colchester Reef lightship back to its station. There was no explanation from the Cambell Brothers, nor was there any apology or even acknowledgement of the vessels damaged by the lightship's absence. As the lightship anchored at its duty post, Captain Bule watched, fuming. It was fortunate that a churning Lake Erie stretched between the enraged master and any associates of the Cambell Brothers.

By Monday the seas had calmed to where a diver could be put over the side to evaluate the ANTELOPE's hull condition, and steam pumps put aboard the wooden steamer in preparation for raising her. Sporting his lead-soled boots and brass diving helmet, Dwyer was helped over the side, as the fresh air bellows pumped in creaking rhythm. The water was cold in the shallows of the reef, but the visibility was nearly perfect. Coming to the boat's giant oak rudder, Dwyer found it badly shattered. Moving lower to the pivot point at the bottom of the rudder, where it is connected to the keel known as the "shoe," he found the structure nearly demolished. Surprisingly, the boat's screw was in fairly good shape. Working along the listing steamer's exposed bottom, he began to take mental notes of the position of each crushed timber and the holes that the rocky reef had stove into the ANTELOPE. He came upon a surprising discovery, one that made him chuckle aloud into his diving helmet . . . the reason the ANTELOPE was caught so firmly on Colchester Reef.

Finishing his survey of the steam-barge's hull, Dwyer was helped back aboard, and must have been still grinning a bit. Briefly he told the gang gathered around him of the damages he had found—and then told them the best part. The reason why the ANTELOPE was snagged so firmly was because she was resting directly on top of the remains of the wrecked tug MAYFLOWER! The machinery of the lost tug had trapped the steamer . . .

With patching gear in hand, the wreck diver went over the side once again and soon the pumps would be put to work. With a burp, a spit, and the hiss of steam, the pumps went after the water in the ANTELOPE. In the space of 15 minutes, the water in the boat was lowered three inches. But, just as the boat appeared to be floating, Lake Erie decided the operation was not to be so easy. Winds began to freshen, the sky again grew dark. As the waves started to roll, the ANTELOPE began to pound, threatening to further wound herself on the MAYFLOWER's bones. The pumping operations halted and the ANTELOPE was allowed to once more settle to the bottom.

For nearly two days, the crew of the ANTELOPE and the wreckers stood by the sunken steamer, waiting for the weather. During that time the tug ERIE BELLE had gathered up the ANTELOPE's loose consorts and taken them to Amherstburg to keep them clear of the storm. On the way off the lake, the ERIE BELLE passed an interesting sight. The light of the Colchester Reef lightship was showing, but from the deck. The lightship's hoisting gear was broken and the lamp assembly could not be raised.

Pumping and lightering of the beaten ANTELOPE resumed on Wednesday, and after an all-night toil by lamplight, the steam-barge was refloated on Thursday, at three o'clock in the afternoon. To put the operation in perspective—the laborers had shoveled 75 tons of coal, by hand, from the ANTELOPE's hold to aid in the salvage. The steamer was towed to Amherstburg where her lightered cargo was reloaded. Her cargo returned, the ANTELOPE departed for a Detroit dry dock in tow of the PRINCE ALFRED, the pumps the wreckers had put aboard her continuously working to expel the lake. When Captain Bule at last got his boat into Detroit, he found there was going to be one final snag. It seems that the ERIE BELLE, with the ANTELOPE's barges in tow, had departed Amherstburg without clearance from Canadian officials. The whole bunch had been seized in Detroit.

In the first five days of November, 1881 the movement of forest products from Bay City was listed in the Bay City Daily Tribune as 12,500 feet of timber; 17,000 feet of railroad ties; lath, 410,000 feet; shingles, 2,080,000 feet; and lumber 22,819,400 board feet. So far, the season had seen 903,181,932 board feet of forest products shipped out. It is little wonder that when the scarred ANTELOPE, sporting 1,000 dollars in repairs as well as the barges COMMODORE, GOULD and PECK, limped into the Saginaw River on November 5th, no one paid much heed. The boats once more mixed in among the trafficking of the river's products. A few days later, the ANTELOPE departed the Saginaw River, now loaded down with a whopping 475,000 board-feet of lumber and consigned again to Tonawanda. Evidently, her rude brush with Colchester Reef had done little to her ability for hauling a load across the lakes in November's chop.

Nearly two years later to the day that it had ensnared the ANTELOPE, Lake Erie more than evened the score with the Cambell Brothers and the lightship that they had chosen so cavalierly to move. On November 11th and 12th, 1883 a severe gale swooped across the lower lakes, and took the Colchester Reef lightship and its master to the depths of Lake Erie.

In the beginning of the 1882 season the ANTELOPE's days as a steamer came to an end. Calculating the expense of operating the little steam-barge, her owners elected to remove the powerplant and convert her to a tow-barge. Once again, the ANTELOPE floated from the shipyard, now at 186 feet and eight inches in length with 523 gross tons burden. Then in 1888, her rig was changed to that of a schooner, presumably to allow her to transport cargo on the rare occasion when a steamer would not be handy. While in tow of the steamer HIRAM W. SIBLEY, off Lake Superior's Apostle Islands, the ANTELOPE's care-worn hull had at last had enough. With the encumbrance of a cargo hold filled with coal, the sad lakeboat's seams simply gave out and she went to the bottom, her crew rescued by the SIBLEY. In retrospect, it seems grossly unfair that after hauling countless tons of assorted cargos over the freshwater seas, the ANTELOPE was so soon forgotten, among the jumble of "king lumber."

Lord Help 'em on the Lakes Tonight

Whenever storm winds blow across the Great Lakes, residents peer from indoor shelter and marvel at nature's power. Those familiar with the big lakeboats and the people who sail on them will view the weather with a special consideration. Thinking of the treacherous white-capped seas and the scores of vessels claimed over the decades, a quiet and informal prayer is whispered into the shrieking wind, over and over . . . "Lord help 'em on the lakes tonight."

The hardwood floor squeaked with each step as Emma Shepard paced about the Bay City office of Henry W. Weber. Hardware purchasing was Mr. Weber's business, and the tidy keeping of his books normally took up Emma's attention. It was Tuesday afternoon, the fourth day of October, 1892, and a bitter wind had been whipping at the office window all morning. Finding every crack around the building, the gusts had turned into a respectable draft, but Emma paid scarce heed to it. Foremost on her mind was the well-being of the wooden lumber hooker NASHUA, and those aboard the steamer.

This was an era of lumber steamers and barges, an era that often confounded the communication contraptions of the day. Boats of the lumber fleet would scurry about, indifferent to the use of the telegraph or that newfangled telephone. With masters of vessels normally owning part or all of their boats, cargos and ports were selected on a whim, or on the rumor of more profit at this port or that. So when Emma Shepard's father, Charles, signed aboard the NASHUA as Mate, she knew that rare would be the times when she would know his whereabouts. Hustling around the lakes, the 135 foot steamer would occasionally hiss its way into Bay City. In that event Mate Shepard would bound into his little girl's workplace or make his way to her Madison Street home for an affectionate visit. It was only then that she was sure where the lumber industry had placed him. When Emma's mother had decided to join Mate Shepard for a bit of autumn pleasure sailing, she too was mixed into the shuffle of "king lumber." Now as the storm winds raged, Emma could only wonder about her parents. Perhaps they were safely tucked in some isolated lumber port, or steaming along some sheltered river. Then again, maybe they were being tossed upon one of the five angry lakes. "Lord help 'em on the lakes tonight," she murmured, chewing the end off yet another pencil.

Aboard the NASHUA was another guest, but his kin were giving far less regard to the current foul weather. They were the relatives of Great Lakes Pilot, 59 year old Captain Archibald Muir. As a career sailor and licensed master of vessels, it was to be expected that Captain Muir would have countless conflicts with wind and wave. Since taking up residence in Port Huron in 1866 the personable captain had become a most popular character, with a reputation for involving himself in any maritime matter that could use his input. A majority of his sailing had been done in and around Georgian Bay and the Canadian shore—in fact it was said in maritime circles that his relationship with those waters was matched by none. Over the years he became also quite an expert when it came to lumber camps, the islands and inlets that surrounded them and the bosses who wheeled and dealed there. Each season he would ship out in the spring and return in the late fall with another year's work done, and fresh tales to keep the neighborhood kids fascinated through the frozen winter days. But after one particularly rough season in command of the barque ACORN, Captain Muir decided to give up full-time vessel mastering. From now on he would hire out his skills as a Great Lakes pilot, sailing only occasionally as a guide through obscure waters. The rest of the time he could rest with his family and friends, and try to catch up on so many months spent at sea.

A founding member of the captains union in Port Huron, Captain Muir would spend hours trading yarns with his peers, and in that contest he had an intriguing tale to tell. With other captains listening intently, Captain Muir would weave the adventure of the barque ALEXANDRIA amidst their cigar smoke. A Scottish immigrant, the good captain had chanced upon the opportunity of guiding the wind-grabber back to his homeland. Leaping at the job, he set sail toward the old country. But while in the western Atlantic, the barque was overtaken by a fierce storm. With all of the anger that the mighty ocean could muster, it took down the ALEXANDRIA's masts and held her at its mercy. In attempting to manage the ship, Captain Muir and three of his crew were swept overboard by a single giant wave and found themselves thrashing about among mountainous foaming seas with the ship the only floating object within countless miles. As the dismasted barque back-rolled down the next wave, Captain Muir and one of the luckiest of the three crewmen managed to grab hold of her rail as it dipped into the sea. Scrambling for their lives, they tumbled back on to the ALEXANDRIA's deck. When the storm abated the survivors jury-rigged a mast and sail and Captain Muir guided the crippled ship into Youghall, Ireland. Repairs made, the lucky captain brought the ALEXANDRIA back to Port Dalhousie without ever seeing his native land.

On the quiet afternoon of Tuesday, September 27, 1892 the tranquility of Captain Muir's Port Huron home

COURTESY MILWAUKEE PUBLIC LIBRARY MARINE COLLECTION

Still showing many of the features of her passenger carrying days,including her multi-sided "Birdcage" pilot house, the wooden lakeboat NASHUA handles coal at the Cleveland Furnace Dock.*

**Author's note: This photo has, in at least one source, been mis-identified as the ATLANTIC. After extensive research with the Instutute for Great Lakes Research and with the Milwaukee Public Library, the author has confirmed without a doubt that the vessel pictured here is the NASHUA.*

was broken by a sharp knock at the door. On the stoop was a Western Union delivery man, telegram in hand. The wire was from Sandusky, Ohio and Captain Decatur Millen of the steamer NASHUA. Captain Millen, it seems, had arranged for a lumber cargo to be brought down from Byng Inlet, Ontario to Toledo, Ohio. The problem was that he had not been up and around that area for some time, so he was bent on chartering Captain Muir's skills as pilot for the NASHUA, and her consort barge the C.N. RYAN.

Captain Muir pondered the request briefly. It had been a long while since he last sailed and it would do him good to once again walk the decks of a lakeboat. He dictated his affirmative response to the delivery man and sent him on his way. Attempting to subdue his growing excitement, Captain Muir dug out his pilot's bag and started packing. Early the following morning, the NASHUA and RYAN arrived at Port Huron and aboard strode Captain Muir with ill-concealed anticipation. By eight o'clock the boats were headed onto Lake Huron and into the crisp autumn morning.

NASHUA was one of a number of former passenger and package freighters, cut down for use in the lumber trade. First enrolled on October 3rd, 1868 the NASHUA was fresh off the builder's ways at the Quelos and Lafrinier yard of Cleveland. A deck house stretched nearly the full length of her 134 foot hull, and within it was a series of passenger cabins. The accommodations for the NASHUA's paying people were spartan by most standards, each cabin sporting a small bed, a table with drawers and a washbowl with pitcher. The cabins were divided by a simple pull curtain that closed the door to a companionway, running the length of the boat. Ahead of the deck house was located a hexagon-shaped "bird-cage" pilothouse, and below deck was a cargo hold suitable for carrying any type of packaged cargo. Overall the boat measured 440 gross tons and was assigned the official number 18537. Her rig was listed simply as "propeller-wood."

From 1868 until 1890, the NASHUA tramped around the lakes hauling passengers and cargo like a water-born stagecoach. Her destinations were often the smaller ports such as Harrisville and Alcona, Michigan. Her job was servicing the lumber camps of Michigan and the people who worked them. In 1881, for example, she is listed as having put into the tiny lumber port of Alcona 27 times. By her

22nd season the boat's small size and lack of elegant fixtures rendered her obsolete for the passenger and freight trade. Also, the lower Michigan lumber camps had started to die out and those that remained were serviced by rail. Once more the boat was being worked over at Cleveland. This time, the middle-most portion of her deck house, as well as the deck that it was constructed upon, was scrapped. All that remained of the deck accommodations was enough aft to house the engine crew and deck hands, and a small portion immediately behind the pilothouse for the captain and mate's quarters. The NASHUA's profile was now that of the standard lakers of the time, and the hold yawned in anticipation of lumber or coal or any other bulk commodity that might be loaded. When she came back out on the 30th of March, 1891, the conversion had given her a reduction in gross tonnage to 298 and a new lease on life.

As the steamer NASHUA and her consort C.N. RYAN crept up Lake Huron toward the entrance to Georgian Bay, Captain Muir joined Captain Millen in the steamer's pilothouse. Ahead, the lake shimmered with a stunning blue-green and Captain Muir paused for a while, just to get reacquainted with his old friend. The NASHUA was running in the service of the Parker and Millen company managed by Captain Millen's brother J.W. Millen. To add to the family strings, the steamer was owned by Captain Richard Millen, Captain Decatur Millen and J.J. McLain, under the flag of the Wolverine Barge Company out of Detroit. Such details were of little concern to Pilot Archibald Muir, his concern centered more around where to stow his gear and what unique qualities were attached to the NASHUA.

Wednesday was taken up by the NASHUA's passage up Lake Huron with the schooner-barge RYAN tugging faithfully at the steamer's stern. Pilot Muir and Mrs. Shepard were not the only extra persons aboard the NASHUA this trip—Captain Millen's wife was along for some pleasure sailing. The only ladies aboard the steamer, Mrs. Millen and Mrs. Shepard had found common ground as the NASHUA moved them around the lakes and had quickly become friends. The two spent hours standing at the boat's rail watching the lake go by and chatting quietly—it was a wonderful escape from the domestic confines of womanhood in 1892.

Dinner time found the NASHUA only a third of the way up Lake Huron and still on course for the entrance to Georgian Bay. Talk over the dinner table probably centered around the technical aspect of sailing into Byng Inlet. The conversation may have extended as far as the passage of the newfangled whaleback steamer PATHFINDER, and her whaleback barge SAGAMORE. It was rumored that the pair was upbound to bring back a record cargo of ore. With the mention of "whalebacks" would come always the debate as to whether or not that was "real steamboating." Boisterous argument mixed with laughter echoed from the NASHUA's galley, and spread across the lake as she plodded silently into the dimming evening.

Wednesday night passed quickly for Pilot Muir. The waves did their job rocking him into a shipboard sleep. Odds are that thoughts of Georgian Bay's rocks and islands, and whether the aging pilot's memory of those waters was good enough to still navigate clear of them, were foremost on his mind. Sleep would be brief, at best.

Rising over the Bruce Peninsula, the orange morning sun found the NASHUA and C.N. RYAN pressing toward the shoal-studded entrance to Georgian Bay. Drifting about the NASHUA's deck houses, the fragrance of bacon, eggs, coffee and other hints of the day's first meal hung like a pleasant fog. Up in the pilothouse two captains stood watch, Captain Millen standing casually, Pilot Muir scanning with keen anticipation the nearing shoreline. In a short time, those tree-carpeted islands clicked in Captain Muir's mind, like the faces of old friends. Apprehension faded without notice, as the pilot busied himself with the NASHUA. Without effort, the NASHUA and her consort passed quietly off Cove Island, Tobermory Point, Flowerpot Island, Bear's Rump Island and all of the rocky shoals that lurk between. It was eight o'clock in the morning, an hour ahead lay Halfmoon Island and 41 miles of open bay before reaching Gereaux Island, and the forested entrance to Byng Inlet.

Georgian Bay, across which the NASHUA and her consort had to pass, is somewhat misnamed. Considering that it measures more than 50 miles wide and over 120 miles long (not including the North Channel which adds an additional 120 plus miles in length), the bay actually resembles an additional Great Lake. The bottom of this "bay-sea" is a jagged series of underwater canyons and boulder-lined pinnacles of doom that seem to jut from the depths in search of unsuspecting vessels. It is not unusual to see the water's depth change from 50 fathoms to five feet, in less than a mile. Such an ice water fang can deliver a mortal wound to a lakeboat, leaving her to sink into the bay's more than 400 foot depth. Without doubt, Pilot Muir's services were needed aboard the NASHUA. Georgian is much more than a simple bay.

It was dinner time Thursday, as the NASHUA and C.N. RYAN eased up Byng Inlet. Pilot Muir had expertly avoided all of the snags and safely led the two lumber carriers to port. Along the way, he had succeeded in refreshing Captain Millen on most of the high spots. On the NASHUA's rail the two lady passengers had stood in awe of the colors among the changing trees. There was deep evergreen blotted with brilliant red, orange and yellow. This was the 1892 version of a color-tour. By the time the two vessels drew near the towering piles of neatly stacked lum-

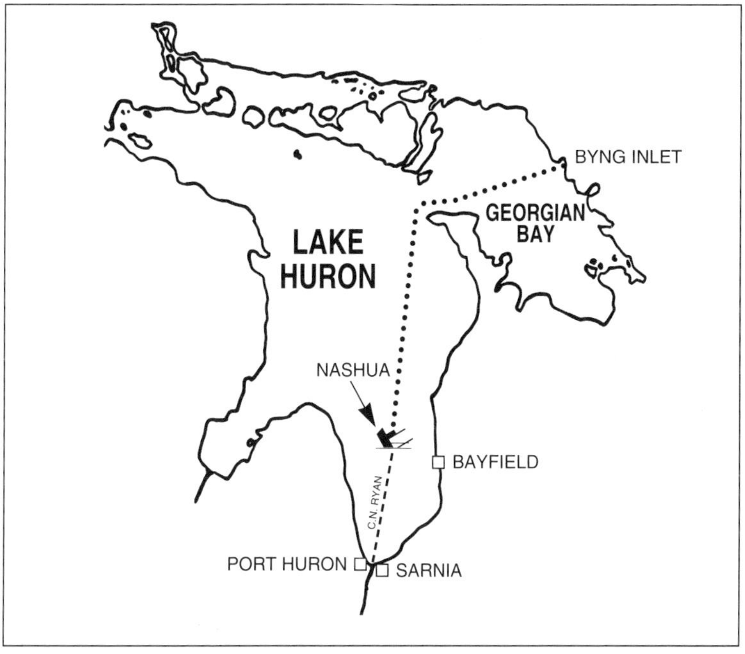

ber there was not enough daylight to start loading. When the opportunity allowed, Captain Miller of the RYAN and Captains Millen and Muir of the NASHUA met dock-side for a bit of master-to-master conversation. It was the first chance in a long while that Captain Miller had to talk with the popular Captain Muir. All three knew that this pleasant trend in the weather was a sign of worse things to come. Autumn's temper was sure to flare and when it did, it would not be a time to be on the open lake. With luck the lumber boats might be loaded and down the lake before that.

The process of loading at Byng Inlet, like everywhere else around the lakes, was tedium—raised to the utmost. Boards of eight and twelve feet in length must be carried up plankways on the shoulders of stevedores and placed aboard each vessel, one at a time. Stevedores alone did not work the loading, as members of the crew were expected to join in the task. With the use of one or two dozen laborers, a boat could be loaded within a day, a genuine accomplishment when considering that the RYAN alone could carry 570,000 board feet of timber product.

Both the NASHUA and the C.N. RYAN were fully loaded by late Saturday. Beginning Saturday morning, however, a heavy northeast gale had been building over all of Lake Huron and Georgian Bay. As the last planks were put aboard, the three captains conferred once again, this time deciding to stay in Byng Inlet and let the storm blow itself out. It was a wise decision, for the weather continued to intensify through the night and blew hard all day Sunday. A massive low pressure system was sweeping down across the southern Great Lakes, with its northern edge bearing the winds of a classic nor'easter. Unknown to anyone on the lakes, an even larger dome of high pressure was charging close behind. The consequences would be a dry, but stiff wind that would switch to the northwest. Without the benefit of any kind of weather reporting or forecasting, the mariners would see only the skies clear and their barometers begin to rise . . . normally a good sign.

At pre-dawn Monday, the stars were twinkling in the Canadian sky and the barometers on the NASHUA and RYAN were on the rise. Winds were still northerly and fresh, but the lumber boats cast off at daylight and headed into Georgian Bay. From atop the RYAN's deck house Captain Miller watched the NASHUA roll as it towed his boat across the open bay. It would be nine storm-tossed hours to open Lake Huron, and the passage through the islands required to get there had claimed many vessels. The crosswind would not help at all, but everyone hoped that by that time the winds would be slacking off.

Shortly before dark, the NASHUA and her consort drew near the thicket of rocks and islands that separates the bay-sea from the expanse of Lake Huron. Climbing once more atop the RYAN's housing, Captain Miller looked again toward the NASHUA. Sky and water were a striking blue—but the wind was howling bitter-cold from nearly due north. Through his binoculars, the RYAN's master could see the seas exploding over the islands to the south. Hunkering down to shelter some behind the RYAN's deck load of lumber, Captain Miller spied the NASHUA. She was blowing good black smoke from her funnel and the wind was streaking it across the water. "Looks like she's makin' good way," he shouted to his wheelsman over the wind, "just follow his line." Rolling like a child's ride at a theme park, the two boats crawled past the islands. By a quarter of six that evening, Pilot Archibald Muir had fulfilled his contract and safely guided the NASHUA and C.N. RYAN into and out of the ordeal on Georgian Bay. It was now Captain Millen's turn to take the pair to Toledo.

Night saw the winds shifting to the north, northwest and aboard the RYAN Captain Miller felt his schooner-barge taking the waves on her starboard stern quarter and cork-screwing in the following sea. This is the worst place to take any kind of sea, but the two lumber boats could do nothing but take the beating. The schooner-barge's master kept a close eye on the deck load and it was riding well, not a single plank shifting out of place. In the hold below, not a drop of water had entered. The RYAN was low and wallowing among the waves, but none were breaking over her, so Captain Miller left the RYAN in charge of the mate, retiring to his cabin, resigned to an uncomfortable, but safe passage down Lake Huron.

Next morning Captain Miller emerged from his cabin as the sky began to turn light. The winds were still strong and a cold October rain met his face. Ahead of the C.N. RYAN, the steamer NASHUA was still rolling heavily in the seas. Looking more closely, Captain Miller noticed that apparently during the night, the steamer's deck load had gone over the side—at least a good part of it was missing. On the other hand, the RYAN's deck load remained in good shape. Flipping up the collar on his heavy woolen jacket, the captain simply shrugged and headed off to breakfast. Lost deck loads were one of the prices to be paid, when hauling lumber on the Great Lakes in autumn.

Captain Miller made short work of what breakfast the RYAN's cook had managed to make. Considering the weather, the cook had contrived another minor miracle in the old wooden barge's "one pot" galley. On deck after only a few minutes in the galley, Captain Miller noticed the RYAN was starting to drift into the trough of the seas. Just after five a.m. Captain Miller, alarmed by the drifting, decided to check on the NASHUA. Clearly, Captain Millen's steamer was adrift as well. No smoke could be seen from her stack and there were no signs of steam at all. The RYAN's master called on all hands to stand ready in the rigging. They would either have to set the storm sails, stand by to aid the NASHUA's crew, or both.

For nearly a full hour the RYAN's crew kept watch over the powerless NASHUA as both boats rolled severely in the waves. At about six o'clock Tuesday morning, October 4th, 1892, the NASHUA let go the towing hawser to her consort barge. With the RYAN still burdened by her deck load, it did not take long for the seas and winds to start separating the two lumberboats. Hindered by the cargo and pitching deck, it took a long time for the sailors to set the sails. By the time the RYAN got running before the winds and had enough way to turn out of the trough, the NASHUA had faded into the waves and rain showers. Without hesitation Captain Miller headed the schooner-barge back in the direction that he thought the steamer might be.

After what seemed like hours, but was actually less than one hour, one of the RYAN's crew began shouting and pointing excitedly. Off to port and slightly behind the schooner-barge the gray silhouette of the NASHUA appeared through the rain. Breaking out his binoculars, Captain Miller got a better look. Rolling nearly on her beam ends and showing no signs of steam, the NASHUA was flying a distress signal.

It was an agonizing moment for Captain Miller. In running before the wind the RYAN had sailed slightly past the NASHUA. Turning any sailing vessel to run in the sea trough toward the NASHUA's position would have required incredible seamanship. Doing the same with the RYAN—sporting a full cargo and deck load with only storm sails set—was simply impossible. Figuring that he was somewhere between Point Clark and Goderich, Ontario, Captain Miller exercised the only option at hand . . . he pressed on toward Port Huron. His hope was to get there quickly and send help back before the NASHUA was blown ashore on the Canadian coast. With any luck, the RYAN might encounter a vessel more able to help the NASHUA along the way, and be able to send help sooner. As the C.N. RYAN moved off to the south, Captain Miller was forced to wonder about the thoughts of Captains Millen and Muir, no doubt watching the RYAN with binoculars of their own. These men were both sailors of great experience who knew well what Captain Miller's options were, so as the RYAN moved off he was doing only what they, under the same circumstances, would have done. (There was doubtless less understanding from the two frightened lady passengers, peering from the cabin windows.) Shortly, the two boats were once again gone from each other's sight.

Hours passed as the C.N. RYAN pounded toward Port Huron with the winds at her heels. About the time that the northwest storm faded to a bluster, Captain Miller spotted the 278 foot wooden oreboat WILLIAM H. GRATWICK. Belching plumes of black smoke that the wind stretched far ahead of her, the GRATWICK was loaded and on the Port Huron course. The RYAN's master knew immediately that without her normal barge in tow, the GRATWICK was quite powerful enough to back-track and pick up the NASHUA. Angling the RYAN toward the steamer, Captain Miller was soon close enough for his megaphone and a call to Captain Peterson of the GRATWICK. Moments later Lake Huron's waves burst against the GRATWICK's white oak bow timbers, showering ice water over her pilot house, as Captain Peterson turned into the seas and charged back to rescue the stricken NASHUA.

Resuming his run, Captain Miller felt a bit better as he watched the staunch steamer, masked in a cloud of black coal-smoke, rolling off toward the Canadian shore. His concern over the fate of his friends aboard the NASHUA unhappily lingered. If she were blown ashore before the GRATWICK could reach her, those aboard could take a savage mauling from the churning surf. The NASHUA was unquestionably far from safe.

At three o'clock Tuesday afternoon the C.N. RYAN sailed into the St. Clair River at Port Huron. No sooner had she made her lines fast to the dock than word of the NASHUA's distress spread through the town. Late in the night the amber lights of the GRATWICK swung past the Fort Gratiot light and she, too, tied up at Port Huron. The crowd gathered around the steamer listened intently to Captain Peterson's story of having searched for nearly four hours trying to locate the NASHUA. All that the GRATWICK found were the waves of Lake Huron and an empty Canadian coast. Darkness had finally forced the steamer to turn and head for Port Huron and it was this report that alarmed the marine community. The following morning a volley of telegrams were sent around the Huron shore. The towns of Goderich, South Hampton, Bayfield and Point Clark all responded. Kettle Point was not contacted, as the fragile telegraph lines running there had been knocked down by the storm.

News of the NASHUA reached the Saginaw River communities and Emma Shepard in the form of a terse story, wired from Port Huron and buried within the local papers on Wednesday. "PORT HURON, Oct. 5.-[Special]-No tidings have been received of the steamer NASHUA. Mrs. Capt. Miller (sic) and Mrs. Capt. Shepard are onboard in addition to a crew of a dozen men. A northwest gale is blowing today." Emma's fears were confirmed. From her accounting desk, Emma felt helpless amid the transpiring events of transporting lumber. Now there was the black feeling that she had lost her parents to Lake Huron.

Long before first light Thursday morning, the tug HOWARD tramped out of Sand Beach heading nearly due east. Salvage was the goal of the tug, salvage and rescue of the missing NASHUA. Today this port, located nearly on the tip of Michigan's thumb, is called Harbor Beach and sees scant vessel traffic. On that blustery Thursday in 1892 it had a different name and was a hotbed of tugs, barges and other vessel traffic on Lake Huron. More than one distressed vessel had been brought into Sand Beach over the years. With fat fees charged and paid for the service, the HOWARD was out for yet another.

By daylight the HOWARD was three quarters of the way across Lake Huron on its search, and in less than an hour's time they came upon the hump of an overturned vessel. All aboard the tug recognized the turtled hull as the NASHUA. Circling gingerly, the tug's crew came upon a shocking sight—the boat's starboard side from 50 feet aft of amidships to the stern was completely gone. The remains of her lumber cargo, trapped within the hold, buoyed the wreck up. There was no sign of survivors, as far as the eye could peer. The HOWARD scrambled back for Sand Beach, arriving at noon with the news.

When the telegraphs at Port Huron began to click with the news of the HOWARD's find, two of Captain Muir's sons, James and Fred, were chartering the tug HAIGHT to start their own search effort. The news served only to hasten their departure, for now they were hoping that the crew of the NASHUA had escaped in the yawl and were camped somewhere on the beach. Arriving on the wreck scene, Fred Muir organized a search patrol of the beaches. The group of locals tramped a forty mile stretch of Canadian shore from Port Franks to Goderich. Their efforts yielded only a pair of life belts that appeared to have once been tied around someone.

By Saturday the wreck of the NASHUA had washed into the shallows three miles south of Bayfield, Ontario, quickly becoming a magnetic tourist attraction. Persons from Port Huron, Sarnia and all along the Lake Huron shore, came to view the luckless steamer . . . now stranded like a beached whale.

Among vesselmen, there grew a consensus as to what had likely happened: as the seas worked the boat's hull, her steam lines had parted, or the seams had opened and flooded her—to the point where the fires were put out. And sometime after the RYAN had left her, as she rolled on her beam ends, the NASHUA's immense iron boiler broke loose of its fastenings. Tossed wildly as the boat rolled, the immense metal cylinder crashed about in the wood-framed engine room, crushing everything in its path. The scene would have been an insane nightmare—with helpless crew scrambling to escape as the boiler charged from one side to the other, like a monstrous steamroller. After smashing the lower deck to toothpicks, it would catapult starboard and drop through the boat's side like a boulder, on the next wave. The boat would have capsized on the spot, taking all aboard.

On Tuesday October 11th, a grieving Emma Shepard received a message requesting that she travel to Brockway to identify the body of her mother—the only one of the boat's people to wash ashore. Pilot Muir, Captain Millen, Mate Shepard and the rest of the NASHUA's souls were the lone witnesses to when and how the boat foundered, but there is one "witness" as to where the NASHUA went over. For over 100 years, the ill-fated steamer's enormous boiler has rested on the bottom of Lake Huron, directly below the precise spot where the NASHUA's people met their end. It lies there at this moment, 14 or so miles off Goderich, alone in the depths, unnoticed and undiscovered. Not glamorous enough a prize to entice research divers and too obscure and deep for amateurs to stumble on, the mammoth cylinder is the sole memorial to the NASHUA . . . and those lost with her.

Dog Barkin'

Within the pilothouse, Captain John Massy was clad only in shirt sleeves, pants and his favorite worn-out slippers as he peered from the open window into Lake Superior's night. For just an instant, he felt a strange presence hovering over his shoulder, as if sensing the gravity of someone who had walked silently close and was now standing behind him. He turned quickly toward the empty presence, half expecting to find one of the crew standing close by in the darkened wheelhouse—but there was no one. An instant later, his attention was drawn to the starboard window where the foggy blackness had suddenly brightened. Before his heart could beat again, Captain Massy was at the whistle pull. Putting his weight to it, he yanked a number of quick tugs commanding his boat's whistle to sound the danger signal. Like a giant freshwater sea monster, another lakeboat rose from the fog, surrounded by the amber glow of her lights, and charged directly at the electrified master's boat. There was time for nothing more than that short danger signal from the boat's whistle, before the two steel lake giants bit into one another with a deafening roar. It became the same scene of horror played too often on the cobalt blue waters off Whitefish Point—the closing act of a story that could be aptly titled "Death of a Lakeboat." Tonight's performance was culminating at midnight, on the ninth day of July, 1911.

This story has its true beginning four years before Captain Massy had that strange feeling and saw the lights in the fog. At the Great Lakes Engineering Works in St. Clair, Michigan, the 440 foot steel hull, designated number

25, hit fresh water. The year was 1907 and hull 25 was christened JOHN MITCHELL. When she entered service the MITCHELL was nothing special to look at. Actually she was just one of a quite common class of oreboats that were rapidly growing in their numbers on the lakes. But to Captain Massy she would soon become both home and office as he guided her up and down the lakes, her hold stuffed with coal upbound, and ore downbound. There was always the autumn opportunity of hauling some late-season grain, but the MITCHELL seemed to be at her best with coal or ore aboard. Such was the boat's lot, and she took to her toil without a whimper each season.

Late in the first week of July, 1911, the 4,468 ton MITCHELL passed from Lake Erie and pounded up the Detroit River. In the boat's cargo hold was piled $35,000 worth of coal bound for Duluth. The vessel was working under the ownership of C.W. Elphicke of Chicago, and standing in command, as usual, was Captain Massy. Taking the better part of a whole day, the steamer snaked her way up the Detroit and St.Clair rivers. Another day was spent huffing up Lake Huron and into the St. Marys River, heading for the Soo. It was a trip that the MITCHELL had made so often that Captain Massy felt that the crew could go ashore and the boat would somehow make the round trip on her own.

Warm and sticky was the air which hovered over Lake Erie and Lake Huron, a thick summer haze squeezing down upon the oreboats as they went about their work. Aboard the JOHN MITCHELL was one group of individuals who were particularly discomforted by July's dog-days. In their full-length long-sleeved white cotton dresses and matching summer hats, were six lady passengers, doing their best to cope with the heat, aided by tall glasses of iced tea and large hand-held fans. From the time they left Cleveland, Mrs. E.A. Smith, Mrs. A.A. Willcutt, and Miss

Clara Bundschuh, along with Mrs. William Grant, Mrs. Albert Grant, and her daughter Alberta, had all sweltered in the smothering humidity. At least young William Grant, who was doing his best to play the part of the ladies' escort to the untamed north, could roll his sleeves up a bit or loosen his collar and still be socially proper. The ladies, however, were not permitted such displays of public laxity on even the hottest days of 1911.

At half past four on the lazy Sunday afternoon of July ninth, in the park adjacent to the locks at the Soo, people had spread elegant picnics upon the grass, as if the scurrying bustle of lake commerce did not exist around them. Quietly the giant steel hull of the JOHN MITCHELL pushed steadily into the lock, the only noise being that of the water seeping through the lock gates. The landing boom would not be invented for another year and a half, so onto the lock wall a pair of deckhands made their way via rope and ladder. The boat's lines in worn hands, the crewmen walked ahead of the steamer as if leading a plow horse. As the MITCHELL entered the lock, the deckhands were joined by the lockmen and together they shouted commands and guided the oreboat into the lock, making her lines fast to the bits. Keeping well ahead of the steamer's motion, the captain already had her engine reversed, and as she came to a near stop the deck crew got her steam winches clanking, to pull the boat the remaining way into the lock. The gates at the lower end of the lock slowly swung closed and the valves under the lock were opened, allowing the higher water above the lock to flow in underneath. The power of countless tons of lake water, bound to seek its own level, began slowly and steadily to lift the MITCHELL. No pumps, no electricity—just the law of physics.

From the MITCHELL's rail, the ladies from Cleveland watched with great curiosity, as the massive steamer was raised effortlessly beneath their feet. As the boat's spar deck rose to a point level with the lock wall, the deck hands stepped casually back aboard. For the ladies, the whole scene was a bit disorienting. The movement of the boat was nearly imperceptible, yet they began to notice that they were looking at their surroundings from a much higher angle. They felt no movement and the only sound was the syncopated clanks of the winches, as the ever-taut lines were let out to compensate for the rising hull. The guests' attention was shifted by young Clara Clemens, the cook's daughter, to the starboard side of the boat, where the rapids of the St. Marys River could be seen in the distance. Shooting down the cascades went a large canoe, with a man paddling each end and a half dozen shrieking tourists seated between. "They're Indians," Clara explained knowingly, "for a dollar they'll run you down the rapids." Watching the soaking that the thrilled canoers were being exposed to, the six proper ladies gasped gleefully and debated whether or not it was worth the price of a dollar.

All at once the entire group was startled, as a single short throaty blast from the MITCHELL's steam whistle split their conversation. It was Captain Massy's signal to all that the boat was prepared to leave the locks. The lines leading aft to the bits on the lock wall were slackened by the steam winches and released by the lockmen. The lines leading forward were left to slack on their own, as the MITCHELL began to inch forward out of the lock, when they too were released from the bits. Billowing a thick black cloud from her giant stack, the steamer began to pick up forward way and slide ahead. The deck winches clanked as steel lines were taken back aboard, and with no more fanfare than that, the JOHN MITCHELL steamed from the western mouth of the canal and on toward Lake Superior.

With a cool, refreshing breeze lofting in off Whitefish Bay, the weather had taken a noticeably pleasant turn. At long last, those aboard the MITCHELL felt some relief from the repressive humidity. Shortly after the MITCHELL left the Soo, cook Al Clemens rang the dinner bell, and everyone not on duty gathered for another of his hearty meals. Aboard the MITCHELL, each repast was a family affair with Al Clemens cooking, his wife serving and his daughter Clara helping where she could. Talk across the dinner table that Sunday evening was largely of the good sleeping weather that the coming night would bring, and all around the boat the mood was as fresh as the gentle breeze that came across the lake.

That same cool breeze which brought a reprieve from the humidity, brought something else. As the sun set, the air grew dense with fog, and the breeze abruptly vanished. The MITCHELL was surrounded by cotton fog, so thick that the after cabins could not be seen from the pilothouse less than 400 feet away. Checking his speed, Captain Massy brought the MITCHELL to a skulk. The boat and crew now became a surreal little world unto themselves . . . there was no radar, radio direction finder or marine radio telephone to break the steamer's isolation. These devices were so far in the future that Captain Massy could not even imagine such things. All he had was his compass and clock, and he was very adept at using them. At the current engine revolutions, he figured the boat's speed at just over three miles per hour, which would put him clear of Whitefish Point at 10 p.m. At that time he would turn to a 294 degree course, bringing him to nearly the center of the lake, some 28 miles abeam of Isle Royale, at about sunset Monday. This calculation was based on the hope that the fog would break by dawn, or that once on open Lake Superior, the MITCHELL would just sail out from under the curtain. In either case, he could increase the revolutions to a good running speed and once again start making good time.

As Captain Massy and the crew groped blindly across Whitefish Bay, many other lakers hauled past them downbound, some seen, most only heard, for like the MITCHELL the fog-shrouded downbounders had their whistles blowing—the standard signal for vessels moving in fog. The problem was that there were many vessels moving across the waters in the vicinity of Whitefish Bay that gray night. Sometimes the air would echo with distant and close whistles overlapping one another, then protracted moments of deep silence, followed by the random whistles once more.

This manner of "feeling" your way instinctively through the restricted waterways of the Great Lakes has long been a skill for which lake mariners have become famous. Salt water sailors who have always relied on volumes of charts, harbor pilots and teams of tugs to find their way, refer jokingly to their Great Lakes counterparts' methods as "dog barking." The implication is that every lakeboat has a dog onboard, and likewise every cabin near every bend along the waterways has a dog. Considering that every dog along the lakes, just like every mariner, supposedly knows one another, the captain of any boat needs only to put his dog at the bow and set that dog to barking, which starts every other dog barking. Now the captain can navigate and avoid other boats by the familiar barking. That is how tightly the Great Lakes sailing community is knitted.

Unfortunately for Captain Massy, the fallacy of "dog barkin'" was nowhere near the truth. There were only the barks of distant steam whistles echoing in the mist. Camouflaged among the distant whistles were the throaty sobs from the whistle of the 376 foot steel oreboat WILLIAM HENRY MACK. In the distance the sound wavered and melted away in the fog. From the MACK's pilothouse window, Captain George H. Burnham was guiding the boat down toward the Soo in the employ of the Jenkins Steamship Company. Setting high out of the water, the MACK was making a rare downbound trip without cargo. Such trips obviously pay nothing, so vessel masters and owners alike were compelled to get them completed and put the next paying cargo aboard as soon as possible. Without doubt, Captain Burnham was motivated to "keep her comin'" down the lake, and was pushing his speed as much as the boat's unburdened status would allow. The fog bank that he had run into at Superior's lower end presented an unwelcome delay, to say the least. Fog meant checking the engine's turns in order to comply with the maritime regulations—Captain Burnham brought the MACK's speed down from sprint to fast walk. Considering the thick conditions this was a token effort at best.

Just before midnight, destiny brought the WILLIAM HENRY MACK and the JOHN MITCHELL together. Like his counterpart aboard the MITCHELL, Captain Burnham had seen the lights appear ahead of the MACK's steering pole an instant before the two oreboats collided. Instinctively, he grabbed the engine telegraph and rang reverse, but before an acknowledgment from the chief could ring back, the two monsters slammed together. So great had been the MACK's forward speed that the impact tossed sleeping crewmen from their bunks. This was no demonstration of prudent checking of revolutions for the current weather conditions.

Most of the MITCHELL's crew, as well as the passengers from Cleveland, were sound asleep when the steamers came crashing into one another. The ladies staggered from their rooms, rubbing their eyes, still half asleep. Reaching the deck, Mrs. Grant found the fog so thick it was nearly impossible to find her way around. From every direction in the dense mist, the shouts echoed and were intermixed with deep groans from twisting hull plates. Shadows of crew members dashed about urgently, their familiar faces obscured by the fog. Somehow, Mrs. Grant was the last of her group to reach the deck, and was now separated from the rest. From the stern, she heard the voice of Captain Massy, urging everyone aft, and she set out stumbling across the deck toward the lifeboat stations atop the stern deck house—clad only in her nightclothes.

Emerging from the Clemens family quarters, young Clara knew just by the tilt of the deck and the frantic actions of the crew that the MITCHELL was sinking. Before she had a chance to be afraid, she was swept up by her parents as the whole family made for the boat deck. As the family hovered near the lifeboat, they could see the crew, who were not working at the life boats, had strung a few lines between the MITCHELL and the MACK. To Clara it must have seemed silly that they were attempting to keep the MITCHELL afloat by using a few skimpy ropes. In actuality, the lines had been rigged as a standby, in the event the steamer suddenly started to go down before the yawls could be swung out. It was hoped that at least some of the crew could scramble across to safety. If this would have worked or not is debatable, but just the effort of rigging the lines must have been a comfort.

A hole large enough to drive a truck through had been punched into the MITCHELL's starboard side, just forward of mid-ship about one third of the way back from the bow. Lake Superior was now cascading into the cargo hold, as if the boat were a thirsty steel monster. The collision with the MACK had inflicted a mortal wound that no power on earth could heal . . . the MITCHELL was doomed. Her own inertia had already torn the MACK loose from the MITCHELL and she was now drifting alongside, her bow ripped open and yawning up to the eight foot mark.

Clara Clemens, with her parents and two crewmen, was placed into one of two lifeboats that had always waited atop the aft deck house. As the boat was being swung out, Al Clemens mumbled something about "the jewelry," bounded from the yawl and stumbled his way into the mist. A moment later the MITCHELL lurched, jarring the lines loose that held the lifeboat. The yawl slammed hard onto the steel deck, so hard in fact, that the impact fractured the leg of Clara's mother. In an instant, the lifeboat tumbled over the side, dumping all aboard 20 odd feet into Lake Superior's frigid soup.

As she came to the surface, young Clara found the yawl floating bottom side up and all of the others clinging to its keel. The two crewmen began thrashing wildly with their feet and uttering loud grunts as they wrestled to flip the lifeboat back over. Quickly taking account of the situation, Clara knew that if something did not change in a hurry some, or perhaps all of those in the water would soon tire and perish in the cold lake. This was especially true of her mother who, suffering with a broken leg, was on the verge of unconsciousness and barely able to keep her head above water. Gazing up the towering steel side of the MACK, she spied several of the crew standing at the rail, feeling utterly helpless. Thinking fast, the plucky young lady conceived a plan, and shouted up to the MACK's crew to throw down a line. Instantly the men began scrambling over one another, and a moment later one of them appeared at the rail with a thick rope. With a splash the line came slapping down just within Clara's reach, and she wasted not a moment in fastening it to the capsized yawl. With the crew of the MACK tugging on the far end and those in the water thrashing and grunting once more, the lifeboat was flipped upright, and the drenched castaways were dragged safely aboard the yawl. As Mrs. Clemens was pulled from the lake, she fainted from exhaustion.

While Clara Clemens' ordeal was being played out down on the lake's surface, Mrs. Grant had managed to fumble her way to the stern, where the crew was gathered around one of the long rung ladders that had been bridged across to the MACK. At the urging of the MITCHELL's crew, the ladies were sent crawling across to the MACK. Unceremoniously, Mrs. Grant was hustled onto the wobbling wooden ladder and with baboon-like posture, began making her way to the MACK. The water was barely visible more than two stories below in the fog and as each of her hands and knees clunked onto the rungs of the ladder, she was sure that at any moment she would surely topple over and be consumed by the misty darkness below. Behind her the death groans of the MITCHELL echoed like a stalking giant and the frantic crew followed as if pursued. She had no time for terror, she felt as if her heart no longer beat, she just closed her eyes and kept crawling hand-and-knee. Suddenly, what felt like a dozen warm burly hands reached out and snatched her from the teetering nightmare. Mrs. Grant was aboard the MACK, safe from the foundering MITCHELL. Right behind her scrambled a traffic jam of crewmen and just as the last of them stepped to safety, the MITCHELL lurched violently, snapping the lines to the MACK like threads, and rolled over and plunged to the bottom—in a hissing whirlpool that turned suddenly into a boiling hill of icy black water.

Hand over hand, the MACK's crew dragged at the rope still attached to the swamped yawl boat, with the remainder of the Clemens family. As they were brought aboard the MACK, young Clara found that her father was not among the survivors clamoring on the deck, and her courage gave way to shock, as she fainted into unconsciousness. The oblivious Clemens ladies, along with all the other ladies, were escorted to the captain's cabin where they remained, as the MACK limped to the Soo.

COURTESY MILWAUKEE PUBLIC LIBRARY MARINE COLLECTION

Seen here in better times, the 440 foot JOHN MITCHELL now rests upside down and imbedded into the mud on Lake Superior's bottom. She is the permanent tomb of her cook who lost his life in an attempt to save his family jewelry.

Sunrise the following morning saw the wounded MACK tied up to the Government Pier at the American Soo, her bow slashed open in a shark-like grin, just above the waterline. All about the decks was scattered the litter of disaster. Jumbles of rope, ladders and lifeboats gave mute account of what had transpired in the cotton fog off Whitefish Point. When the MITCHELL died she took only three of her crew with her: Second Mate Archie Causley, Watchman George Austin and Cook Al Clemens. That fact alone said much about the brave work of all who had been involved. The weeks and years ahead would see certificate action against both masters, along with finger-pointing and the usual claims against both shipping companies. All this a result of one night—when the dogs just were not barkin'.

The wreck rests today upside down in 150 feet of water, her cabins crushed into the muddy bottom by the weight of the massive hull. It is a haunting display in the ice water museum, where Al Clemens traded his life to become permanent custodian of a few jewels . . . forever entombed in the overturned hull of the JOHN MITCHELL.

An Arched Ship in the Ice Water Museum

Almost at the tip of Michigan's thumb is a tiny port town known as Harbor Beach, built there because into the shoreline, nature has cut a natural shelter from Lake Huron's hair-trigger temper. Today coho salmon fishermen and other sport fishermen depart from the port every day that the weather permits, to toss their lines into the fresh water and relax by waiting for that big fish to grab the line. Standing on the shore or breakwater, one can see the sport boats spreading toward the horizon for miles. Crawling along that same distance are the giant steel oreboats, moving silently on the prescribed upbound and downbound courses. What is not seen is a single, small wooden steamboat, with tall arches on her beams and a bird-cage pilothouse. Through the fishing season, the shipping season and the winter months when the lapping waves turn to ice, the old boat goes unnoticed, as she has for over 100 years. Unnoticed—because she rests in the deep dirty darkness on the floor of Lake Huron.

There were a few hours that needed to pass before dawn would brighten the Detroit and St. Clair rivers, and the 17 mile stretch of shallow Lake St. Clair that lies between. As the little steam-barge EAST SAGINAW thrashed her way onto open Lake St. Clair, Captain Richardson squinted ahead into the sackcloth darkness. It was Monday morning the 24th day of September, 1883 and the EAST SAGINAW was upbound, light, pulling a string of four barges. Ahead was the normal spattering of dim amber lamps, most on vessels, and a few on the distant shore. Through the darkness two sets of lights caught the captain's attention, apparently a pair of lakeboats approaching to pass, so Captain Richardson grabbed the boat's whistle pull and sounded the passing signal. Moments later, the opposing steamer answered with a melodious and familiar toot. Smiling a little, Captain Richardson pulled again at the whistle, this time sounding a brief salute which was promptly echoed back. The oncoming steamer was the BAY CITY, sistership to the EAST SAGINAW, bound out of her namesake port with the schooner-barge THEODORE PERRY in tow.

Born at the McDole yard in Marine City, Michigan in May of 1866, the EAST SAGINAW was another of the workhorse steamers to start her career there. These boats grew from the technology on hand at the time, so their hulls were those of the sailing vessels of the day, but every other feature of the boats was not much to look at. In fact, they were downright homely. At the rearward most part of the hull, the boat's steam engine was placed, and stuck through the boat's heels was the propeller. Plopped upon the deck over the engine works, almost as an afterthought, was the deck house and atop it a multi-sided bird cage pilothouse and a tall smoke stack. Hulls such as the EAST SAGINAW's were about 150 feet long and around 13 feet in depth, and those who considered themselves marine architects felt that such a hull would flex in a heavy sea. So, giant arches were constructed on the boat's beam, arcing from the area of the forward mast to nearly halfway past the deck house. These "hogging arches" were quite common in lake vessels of the 1860s and early 1870s. (In later years, they were found to have no real effect on the boat's structure, and were no longer seen on new vessels.) Little, powerful steamers of the EAST SAGINAW's class, were not very elegant in appearance and were soon dubbed "steam-

Small steamers such as the EAST SAGINAW became a common tool for moving cargos across the lakes in the 1880s. There are no known photos of this boat and she has yet to be found, so this author's drawing gives a general impression of the boat.

barges," perhaps to denote the general disdain for them among the more aristocratic marine buffs.

When it came to appearance, the EAST SAGINAW was far from a sleek beauty. A cross between a barge, a tug, and a bulk carrier, the 235 ton steamer was a true ugly duckling. When her younger sister, the BAY CITY, came out of Marine City a year later, aside from being 137 tons greater in burden, she was just as homely. By 1883, however, the BAY CITY had suffered a bad fire and was rebuilt with more modern upper workings. Now she and the EAST

SAGINAW were running together on the Saginaw to Cleveland route, hauling lumber for the Cleveland and Saginaw Freight Lines.

Normally, lakeboats of the 1800s made the best of their travels by carrying a cargo, any cargo, on each leg of a trip. The concept of running down the lakes with cargo and returning light, or empty, did not come into vogue until World War II, but the contract of the Cleveland and Saginaw Freight Lines was so profitable, the toil of the EAST SAGINAW and BAY CITY was simply to haul lumber down and scurry back, light, for yet another load. This was a repetitive shuttle that those aboard the C. & S.F.L. boats did not mind one bit. Once a week, they were either in Cleveland or Saginaw or in between, unlike their counterparts in the lumber trade who tramped about the lakes at the whim of the lumber barons.

What remained of Monday's pre-dawn hours and Monday morning, was spent by the EAST SAGINAW pulling her barges up the St.Clair River. A weary Captain Richardson spent the time between downbounders leaning at the open pilothouse window, watching the riverside villages pass, while the gremlin of sleep tugged at his sleeve. Just past noon, the confines of the river suddenly opened ahead of the EAST SAGINAW, and Captain Richardson swung the steamer and her tail of barges on the normal upbound course. He gave First Mate Tom Fitzsimons the order to start paying out the towing hawser, from the short length used in the winding river, to the distance best for open lake. That task finished, the mate returned to the pilothouse and the captain gave him charge of the boat, and went to his cabin for some well-earned sleep.

Bringing the EAST SAGINAW up from Port Huron was a familiar task for Mate Fitzsimons, because Captain Richardson normally gave him the boat as they reached the open lake. On his way to his room, the captain stopped by the boat's snug galley. This was the realm of Steward William Eccles and his son William Jr. As it was the mate's job to take the steamer when the captain handed it off, it was the job of William Eccles to command the boat's big iron cook-stove. Doubtless, as he made his way to his cabin, Captain Richardson felt assured that all aspects of the EAST SAGINAW were in good hands.

Sleep for the captain was not long lasting. A few short hours after he put his head to the pillow, the EAST SAGINAW began to pound, jarring him awake. Returning to the pilothouse, he saw that the mate had things well in hand, but the wind was rapidly freshening out northwest. At this time, the EAST SAGINAW's design itself was the problem. There was no such thing as ballast tanks, and the steam-barge, running without cargo, had most of her hull out of the water. With her bow out of the water nearly to the keel, the boat was an easy target for the developing storm, but it was also a characteristic of the boat's design that provided the solution to this dilemma. Her extremely shallow draft would allow Captain Richardson to run up close to the shore and stay in its lee, until he could make the mouth of Saginaw Bay, or if things worsened, he could duck into Sand Beach harbor.

As the storm grew in intensity, the five lumber boats held their own, sheltering beside Michigan's thumb. With the winds blowing over 35 miles per hour, the crafty master had found the ideal way to run with his boat. As so often happens on the Great Lakes, if the freshwater's temper cannot get you one way, it will get you in another. So it would be with the EAST SAGINAW. Just after Captain Richardson had made the decision to by-pass Sand Beach and keep heading up to the mouth of the Saginaw Bay, the steam-barge jolted sharply, nearly tossing the three men in the pilothouse to the deck. In the galley, steward Eccles was juggling like a circus performer, in a vain attempt to

COURTESY MILWAUKEE PUBLIC LIBRARY MARINE COLLECTION

Sister ship to the EAST SAGINAW, the BAY CITY is seen here after her deck houses were burned and reconstructed. The BAY CITY clearly shows her arches in this photo.

grab tumbling dishes. The EAST SAGINAW had found a reef just off Sand Beach.

For a moment it felt as if the lake had delivered only a glancing blow, but it soon became clear that the EAST SAGINAW was fetched up solid on Crane's Point. "Get down there and cut loose the barges, Tom," the master ordered, with a resigned groan. It was the correct move to make, the schooner-barges would be much better off on their own, than leashed to the stranded steamer. And if the tethered barges were to be caught by the wind, they would grind the steam-barge's hull on the rocks. In no time at all the EAST SAGINAW was free of her burden and on her own—perched on the boulders nearly within wading distance of Sand Beach Harbor.

A quick inspection of the boat showed why all the attempts to maneuver off the shoal had been fruitless. The boat's screw had been wrecked and her rudder unshipped. There was no use in further attempts to maneuver. It would take a tug to pull her off. Quickly it was decided to send a man ashore to enlist such help. Even with the storm winds blowing, the seas were still low enough to allow the steamer's yawl to reach Sand Beach, so it was readied to go over the side. Captain Richardson put the yawl in charge of Mate Fitzsimons, along with two of the crew and sent them on the long, cold row to the harbor to charter a tug. It took some doing, but Fitzsimons got the yawl into Sand Beach, and slogged his way around the docks. The captain had specified that he wanted the tug KELLOGG chartered and Fitzsimons found it and stomped aboard. Drawing twelve feet in depth, the KELLOGG would be in danger of putting herself aground and her master flatly refused to go out after the EAST SAGINAW, reckoning her to be in shallower water. Now the EAST SAGINAW's mate began a hurried search about the harbor, in quest of a tug to go to his boat's aid.

It seemed like a week had passed, until the yawl with Fitzsimons aboard came beating back out to the EAST SAGINAW. Captain Richardson had taken a hard chance, in dispatching the small boat. The yawl was the one lifeboat for the crew, should the steamer start to break up on the rocks, and the captain had gambled that either Fitzsimons would return, or a tug would be out, before that happened. But the soaking wet first mate came dripping into the pilothouse and reported to Captain Richardson—there would be no tug.

Why the tugs refused to come out that night remains unclear. Some sources claimed the weather was too rough, but traditionally tug captains have challenged the lakes at their worst, for just the hint of a towing fee. And if Mate Fitzsimons was able to row the yawl from the EAST SAGINAW to the port and back, just how rough had the weather been? More likely, either the boat was in waters too rocky and shallow to risk a tug, or Captain Richardson made a monetary offer too low to motivate the tug captains. Perhaps a combination of these reasons was to blame. Whatever the conjecture, the EAST SAGINAW appeared to be left on her own.

Shortly after the mate had broken the bad news to Captain Richardson, the dim amber lamps of a small tug came rolling out of the harbor. Evidently the master of the tiny tug ADAMS had decided to take a pull at the beleaguered EAST SAGINAW. With the winds snatching and the rains pelting at their efforts, the tug's crew made a number of efforts at casting a line into the wind at the EAST SAGINAW, but it was apparent that there was no way to get a line aboard. The tug ADAMS gave up and steamed back into port. This aborted effort was another indication that those ashore did not seem to feel the EAST SAGINAW to be in any immediate danger. If there was dire peril, the tug at least would have stood by the steambarge.

Midnight came and went and the EAST SAGINAW ground her bottom on the rocks, but seemed to be holding together. The lights of her barges, safely anchored beginning about three miles south of the steamer's location, could be clearly seen rolling in the distance. The winds began to blow harder, gusting in excess of 50 miles per hour. Now the Michigan shore could no longer provide enough lee to protect the wooden steam-barge, and the EAST SAGINAW began to drag off the shoal. Just before two o'clock Tuesday morning, with a series of groaning crunches, the steamer was ripped from the reef and seized by the wind.

Her screw damaged and her rudder shipped, the little lakeboat was powerless and was being carried onto the open lake. The logical step would have been to drop the anchors, bringing the boat into the wind to ride the storm out. Instead, the captain started blowing distress signals, in hope of drawing a tug to the rescue, or attracting the attention of the normally vigilant lifesavers. Within the boat's cargo hold, cascades of water began to spout. Apparently the rocks had parted a large number of the boat's hull timbers when she was blown from the reef. Moments after the steam-barge started rolling free, Mate Fitzsimons again slogged into the pilothouse and informed the captain in no uncertain terms that the EAST SAGINAW was sinking. Captain Richardson responded with renewed distress signals.

Crewmen were put to work at the boat's pumps and three of the crew went at bailing from the forward hatchway, and five at the aft hatch. Below in the engine room the firemen and engineer worked at bailing the fire hold and ash bucket. Their efforts were in vain as the lake gained rapidly on the desperate crew. The intruding lake had over-run the engine room, replacing her fires with frigid water. Her steam supply knocked out, the boat's heat supply was gone. But there was no time for shivering as the crew bailed for all they were worth—while the EAST SAGINAW drifted into the blackness of Lake Huron.

The seas were not breaking over the helpless steam-barge, but the swells were very high, and through the night the lake steadily devoured the leaking hull. The water in the hold became too deep for the bailing crew to keep their footing among the sloshing flood, so the crew bailed from the rolling deck as the boat continued to settle there about three feet. Working with all their strength, the crew felt as if they were keeping the steamer afloat, but in actuality they might as well have been using tea cups to bail . . . Lake Huron was not about to give up the EAST SAGINAW and as dawn approached, was threatening to take the lakeboat and all aboard her.

By daylight, the water was up to the boat's spar deck and Captain Richardson got that urgent feeling that the boat might now plunge suddenly to the bottom. He shouted to Fitzsimons to stop bailing and take to the boat. Over the rail the yawl was passed, and into it piled the 12 exhausted crewmen. Last to leave the EAST SAGINAW were Mate Fitzsimons and Captain Richardson. In lee of what small portion of her hull remained above water, the castaways clung to the settling boat. With 14 men in the yawl, about the stature of a large rowboat, there was only about six inches of freeboard out of the water. Swamping of the lifeboat would be a very real possibility, if rowing were attempted. Mindful of this, the soaked, shivering crewmen hung onto their sinking shelter.

It was all the crew could manage just to keep the crowded yawl afloat, when what had been a smudge on the morning horizon started to take shape, and the familiar outline of the big wooden package steamer CONEMAUGH became clear. Shouting and waving for all they were worth, the castaways were answered by a throaty series of blasts from the CONEMAUGH's whistle. From the package freighter's pilothouse, Captain Cochran had spotted the sinking EAST SAGINAW, with only her arches, funnel and pilothouse above the rolling waves. As he closed on the wreck, he saw the tiny boat cast off and begin to drift away in the gale.

Easing the CONEMAUGH between the EAST SAGINAW and the yawl, Captain Cochran used the freighter's 258 foot oak hull to block the wind. As the CONEMAUGH came to a stop, her crew opened the boat's big wooden side-ports. With the package freighter rolling heavily, lines were tossed and ladders lowered as the wallowing yawl drew close up under the CONEMAUGH's hull. One by one the shipwrecked crew clambered to safety. Only two were left, when the yawl was slammed by the package freighter's guard and suddenly capsized—tossing them both into the lake nearly beneath the giant lakeboat. One of the two got to the CONEMAUGH's aft gangway and was pulled from

COURTESY MILWAUKEE PUBLIC LIBRARY MARINE COLLECTION

The big wooden package freighter CONEMAUGH came to the rescue of the EAST SAGINAW. Through her side gangways, (visible in this photo) the crew was plucked from Lake Huron.

death. The second, William Eccles Jr., was swept into the heaving waters.

Garbled shouts were all the others heard as the unlucky lad seemed to vanish among the swells. Kicking and thrashing in the icy water, Eccles clawed to keep his head above the waves. Being dunked constantly, with water shooting up his nose, he could catch only a glimpse or two of the CONEMAUGH and to his horror he saw black smoke belch from her stack, as she began to move away. Certain that he had been left for dead, William Eccles Jr. tried to shout with rage, but the CONEMAUGH moved farther off. The water numbed his hands and feet and his clothing weighed him down as if woven of lead. In the distance the EAST SAGINAW was no longer visible among the giant swells, and the shipwrecked sailor found himself bobbing helplessly, more than six miles from land.

As the disheartened castaway was about to give up to Lake Huron, he caught a glimpse of the CONEMAUGH with her beam now to him. The package steamer was turning in the storm, and coming back for him, but the water was frigid and he could now barely feel his arms and legs. From the CONEMAUGH's pilothouse Captain Cochran, flanked by Captain Richardson and Mate Fitzsimons, skillfully maneuvered his boat in the giant seas. At her wooden rail stood the entire crew of the EAST SAGINAW, and that of the CONEMAUGH, scanning the waves for their lost compatriot.

Rolling madly with the wind screaming among her wires, the CONEMAUGH made a wide circle and headed back toward where the unfortunate crewmen had been carried off. Turning a big lakeboat under the conditions that existed on Lake Huron that morning, was no small task in itself. Finding a drowning man in miles of open, heaving lake bordered on the impossible. Luckily for William Eccles Jr., no one had told Captain Cochran that. Crates and casks were flung helter-skelter in the steamer's hold, and her hull timbers wailed in protest, as the CONEMAUGH pulled around to oppose the crazed water. Smashing through the waves, the package freighter punched into the spitting wind, fighting for the life of a single man.

Meanwhile down the lake, at Port Huron, the twin-stacked sidewheel passenger steamer CITY OF MACKINAC edged up to the Wright and Eldridge dock. Through cupped hands, the master of the spanking new steamer shouted to the dock that the steamer "SAGINAW CITY" had gone ashore at White Rock, Michigan, floated free, and sunk at about half past six that morning, nine miles off-shore and five miles down from Sand Beach. When voices from the dock called back questions, and if the CITY OF MACKINAC had bothered to try and help, the captain simply shouted that the lifesavers had rowed out and picked them up. With that he slipped back into his pilothouse and closed the door.

The report spread like wildfire, only logical because it was almost completely inaccurate. But it is a good question to ask—why the captain of the CITY OF MACKINAC had such details but rendered no aid. His boat must have passed close enough to the foundering EAST SAGINAW to size up the situation, and that must have been before the CONEMAUGH appeared on the scene. Otherwise, why use the lifesavers as an excuse for passing up a lakeboat in distress? Never mind, the CITY OF MACKINAC would be on her way back to St. Ignace at four o'clock the next afternoon, long before anyone could put the pieces together and start asking questions the captain wished to avoid.

Late Tuesday afternoon September 25th 1883, the package steamer CONEMAUGH marched into Port Huron. In her pilothouse was a satisfied Captain Cochran, satisfied because warming in the boat's cabins was the entire crew of the ill-fated EAST SAGINAW. Included was William Eccles Jr. who, being treated to hot food and a bit of strong spirits, was recovering just fine. Whether it was divine intervention, pure chance or incredible skill will never be known, as the captain had guided the steamer directly to the benumbed crewman, and he had been plucked at the last moment from the lake's cold beckon.

Captain Richardson wasted no time in publicly chastising the Sand Beach tugs and lifesavers for not coming to the assistance of the crippled EAST SAGINAW. His comments went unanswered, and were drowned out by the clamor of the shipping industry. Weeks passed, and the captain's anger was forgotten . . . years past and the EAST SAGINAW was forgotten, too. On June 12th, 1892, less than a decade from the EAST SAGINAW's sinking, her sister ship BAY CITY burned to an end in the Rouge River at Detroit. By the early 1900s, all of the steam-barges of the 1860s were extinct.

Nowadays, vessels with all cabins stacked aft are again tramping the surface of the Great Lakes. The port of Sand Beach has long been renamed Harbor Beach, and is too small for the giant modern lakeboats to normally seek shelter in. All that seems to remain of the arched wooden steam-barges are some cluttered old photographs, but there are actual examples of these old boats, in cold storage around the lakes. One of these rests more than 100 feet below the surface, between six and eight miles southeast of the Harbor Beach breakwater, preserved in the ice water museum's Sand Beach exhibit. Here rests the EAST SAGINAW, as she has for more than a century. Steward Eccles's big cook stove and pots and pans are still in the galley as he left them. All about the hold are the implements used in the useless effort to keep the boat afloat, covered with a bit of silt, undisturbed. This attraction has yet to be opened to the public, since the EAST SAGINAW has, as of this writing, not been found by research divers. She seems to be waiting, perhaps in the hope that the powers-that-be will legislate the protection of all the Great Lakes bottom lands, and protect her and her kin from the ghouls in wet suits that would strip her to the planks. Seasons will come and go, the lake will freeze and thaw, the giant steel oreboats will pass overhead . . . the EAST SAGINAW will lie in wait below, one more exhibit in the ice water museum.

Signed Patrick Howe

It was a fair autumn day when Patrick Howe popped through the door of the John S. Parsons ship chandlery down on Water Street in Oswego, New York. Normally Parsons' establishment was a center of traffic for those who docked in the port as well as the local telegraph office, but Patrick was not there to send a wire. The ring of the bell above the door attracted the attention of merchant Parsons, who clopped forward across the worn hardwood floor. Much to his surprise, the storekeeper found not a customer, but his new friend Mr. Howe, standing at the counter with a large painting tucked under his arm.

As Mr. Parsons approached, Patrick held out the painted canvas for the merchant to admire. "It's fer you," the amateur artist said, "I painted it, it's the river here in Oswego." Mr. Parsons happily accepted the painting and promptly posted it where every customer could appreciate it. Parsons was a collector of amateur art, and boat models that those who sailed the lakes were fond of producing, and this would be a welcome addition to his private ice water museum.

Patrick Howe had not been long in the Oswego area and his current employment as cook onboard the steamer HOMER WARREN kept him moving in and out of that port. Before that he had sailed the saltwater seas, but the jumble of the First World War had brought him to the lakes. Except for those aboard the boat, he had few friends in his newly-adopted home, but did make the acquaintance of merchant Parsons, and every time the WARREN put her lines out at Oswego, Patrick made his way to Parsons to

COURTESY MILWAUKEE PUBLIC LIBRARY MARINE COLLECTION

Sporting the lines of a typical lumber hooker, the HOMER WARREN spent most of her career shuttling freight on the lower lakes. It was hauling coal to Canada that filled her hold until the end of her days.

buy supplies for his galley and engage in some friendly conversation. This was the era when a friendly neighbor could stroll into a store and just stand about chatting with the owner. It was the autumn of 1919.

Hunched beneath the coal docks at Oswego, the 180 foot wooden lumber hooker HOMER WARREN was opening her hatches to take on 494 tons. It was the 25th day of October, and the boat's cargo was Toronto-bound under the supervision of Captain William Stocker, a resident of the city. Sailing aboard the WARREN, as with many small wooden lakeboats of her breed, was largely a family affair. Serving aboard Captain Stocker's boat as mate was his brother George, and an even larger family group was preforming duties in the boat's engine room. There was Chief Engineer William Kerr, who with the captain owned shares in the boat, and under his supervision were his brothers George and Joseph, working as fireman and second engineer respectively. These two families, with cook Patrick Howe, deckhands Stanley Foste and William Talbot, comprised the crew of the HOMER WARREN. As the boat waited her turn to take on coal, Patrick Howe stood at the rail just outside the door of his galley, gazing across the river and pondering his next painting. Overhead, the fair sky misrepresented the weather pattern forming to the west, and brightened the harbor scene in a manner that he found inspiring.

More than a half century before that inspirational Saturday, the Cleveland shipyard of Peck and Masters launched the fine wooden passenger vessel ATLANTIC. The year was 1863 and the ATLANTIC embarked on a career hauling passengers and packaged cargo around the freshwater seas. Like others of her day, the boat had passenger accommodations planted atop a cavernous hold, accessed via side-ports and capped, as usual, with a bird-cage pilothouse from which the boat would be guided. Her safe operation would be overseen by a hand-carved wooden eagle mounted proudly atop the pilothouse. The single tall mast standing behind the pilothouse could be fixed with a sail to augment the ATLANTIC's steam engine.

By the turn of the century the ATLANTIC's marginal size and antiquated accommodations had banished her to the lay-up wall. It was then that the wizard of wooden lakeboats, James Davidson, contracted her for conversion to a lumber-carrier. At Mr. Davidson's West Bay City yard the tired old ATLANTIC had her passenger quarters stripped, her sides brought up a foot and a half, the beam widened two feet and hull configured for lumber and general bulk cargos. She sailed from Bay City sporting the typical lumber hooker profile and a new name, HOMER WARREN. Shortly thereafter, the WARREN was wed to the three-masted 170 foot schooner-barge IDA KEITH. On October 26th, 1902, the pair were in Bay City, this time after being sold at the U. S. Marshal's auction to James Davidson, and from then on they seemed forever to be related to the Saginaw River area. For years, the pair was seen on the lakes as steamer and consort. In the spring of 1919, Toronto vesselman J.P. Milnes engaged the WARREN and brought her to Lake Ontario, to serve in the shuttling of coal between Oswego and Toronto.

Making frequent trips, the WARREN's routine allowed her crew to plan around the schedule in much the same way as a passenger boat. This was a luxury that many who sailed the lakes were not afforded, but as people are wont to do, they soon took the WARREN's routine for granted. On this, the last Saturday in October, Chief Kerr had counted on the steamer getting away with her cargo in the first hours of Saturday morning, putting them in Toronto about 22 hours later. Plenty of time to grab a little sleep, muster his brothers from the boat and help his wife move their possessions while the WARREN was unloading. Unfortunately for the chief, his well-formed plans were run aground, as Saturday dawned and the WARREN sat waiting her turn at the J.B. McMurrich coal trestle. After a brief conference with First Mate George Stocker, it became clear to the chief that the WARREN might be delayed until Wednesday morning. Considering this, Captain Stocker told his good friend Chief Kerr to catch the train to Toronto, and if he could get back before the WARREN sailed, fine. If not, the boat would surely survive one trip across the lake with only two Kerrs aboard. With the prodding of the ship's officers, the chief hurried off for the Toronto train.

Monday evening found the WARREN finally taking on her coal burden and short one hand, Chief Kerr. Fortunately, the hiring of temporary crewmen along the Oswego waterfront in 1919 was quite easy, and shortly Second Engineer Joseph Kerr had rounded up two able bodies for the WARREN's firehold on the trip to Toronto. The dock workers that evening had overheard one of the two men give his name simply as "Thompson" and nobody could recollect the name of the other man. With a crew of eight the WARREN was considered fully staffed, although the crew was about half of most vessels of her class. In these days before seaman's unions and regulated working shifts, many of the crew would have to pull double duty—but the boat would make money shuttling coal.

Shortly before four o'clock Tuesday morning, the wooden laker HOMER WARREN took up her lines and headed out onto Lake Ontario. With Captain Stocker standing in command of the pilothouse and his brother George trading his duty of first mate to take his turn as wheelsman, the steamer was soon clear of the river channel, and in deep enough water to turn on the normal track for Toronto. Picking up the normal loaded pace of just over six miles per hour, it took less than an hour before the WARREN's lights had been swallowed up in pre-dawn blackness. Should the schedule be kept, the WARREN would be delivering her coal and picking up her absent engineer in just under 24 hours.

With the rising sun, came the rising winds from Lake Ontario. As the businessmen around Oswego turned their "closed" signs around to the "open" side, they were met with a truly foul day. Along the river the vesselmen put out extra lines and braced for some stiff weather—exactly what they would get. No sooner had this stormy business day started, than the telegraph at the Parsons ship chandlery began clicking feverishly. The wire was from Chief Kerr in Toronto, asking if the WARREN had departed yet and stating if she had not, he could be in Oswego by evening to re-join the crew. Mr. Parsons wired back a brief response stating that the WARREN had sailed and that a storm was blowing at Oswego. Receiving the reply, chief Kerr returned to his residence, planning to meet the boat Wednesday morning while she was unloading.

Apple farmers along Lake Ontario's southern shore, many of whom had yet to bring in a substantial portion of their crop, witnessed the autumn winds blast through their orchards. The blasting torrents of frigid wind ripped the unharvested fruit from the trees, and finished the harvest for the farmers. Throughout the morning, the low gray sky boiled with dark clouds racing southward off the lake as the wind continued to howl with increasing temper.

Just west of Sodus, New York, a farmer was making his way back to his house near Bear Creek, when he paused to scan the enraged lake. The normal gem-blue color had been replaced with storm cloud gray, and the rolling surface had taken on the image of broken glass, as sharp, heaving waves jutted toward the sky. Along the beach, big breaking seas pounded the sand—the whole scene was fearful. To the west on the ill-defined horizon, an object became clear among the peaks of the seas, and caught the farmer's eye. It was a lakeboat headed east toward either Sodus Bay, or Oswego. As he watched the shadowy image spewing streaks of smoke from her funnel, it is likely that the farmer felt a bit of pity for those aboard her, tossed by the lake. Turning his back to the wind and trudging toward his own doorstep, he probably could not understand why someone would want to make a living out on that lake. Opening his door, the farmer had the distinct impression that he heard the repeated toots of a distant steam whistle, but between the wind whipping the brim of his hat and the roar of the surf, it was hard to tell. Glancing at the kitchen clock, he took notice that it was just after 10 o'clock—and knowing he had much to do, the farmer pushed his way back outside. At that moment he glanced back toward the lake and noticed that the lakeboat was nowhere to be seen. As he went about his chores through the stormy day, the disappearance of the steamer—and that faint whistle—nagged at him.

At Ogdensburg, New York, the storm interrupted the normal ferry service across the lake, and at Cape Vincent the dock was completely swallowed by the in-rolling waves. In that same city Coon's big riverside warehouse was set upon by the seas that reached half-way up the four-story structure, shattering windows and sloshing through doorjambs. Much of the cheese that was stored in the building was tainted by the intruding lake and subsequently turned into a smelly moldy slime. Out at the Cape breakwater more than a dozen lakers were shielding themselves from the waves. And so it went through the night . . . but by dawn the storm eased and Lake Ontario began to subside.

Early Wednesday morning the phone at the J. B. McMurrich Coal Company rang, splitting the early morning hush. It was the Coast Guard calling from Sodus. Apparently guardsmen had found two bodies and a large clutter of wreckage strewn along the west side of Sodus Point. The two floaters were wearing life preservers marked "CITY OF GRAND RAPIDS" on one side and "HOMER WARREN" on the other. The word of this baffling puzzle spread wildly around the Oswego river-front, but marine men in the know quickly pointed out that the only CITY OF GRAND RAPIDS was currently sailing for the Graham & Morton fleet out on Lake Michigan. Apparently, the life belts found on the drowned crewmen were second-hand equipment, from a former boat of the same name. There was little doubt that the bodies and the wreckage were from the WARREN.

Once again, a wire was dispatched from Mr. Parsons to the Milnes Coal Company of Toronto regarding the WAR-

REN. Just as the wire was received, Chief Kerr shuffled casually into the office to inquire as to the delay in his boat's arrival. He had fully expected to see her at the coal dock. The ashen faces in the office told him in an instant that something was wrong. With a trembling hand, Mr. Milnes passed the telegraph message to the frightened chief engineer—who read it . . . and collapsed.

More word was received from Sodus Wednesday evening. At three o'clock that afternoon Lake Ontario surrendered two more bodies, and from the papers in their pockets they were positively identified as the Kerr brothers, George and Joseph. Together at the end, they had come ashore surrounded by bits and pieces of the WARREN, including a sea-chest, some pictures, and some broken oars. Receiving this word, Chief Kerr and Mr. Milnes boarded the train for Oswego to bring home their people.

Through the night, flotsam washed ashore, along Sodus Point and as far west as Pultneyville. Oars, pieces of the WARREN's pilothouse, a refrigerator, a shattered lifeboat with a hole in it . . . all were tossed onto the beach in the same area as the four luckless crewmen. Shortly after the wreckage washed up, the winds shifted to blowing from the south, preventing any further debris from coming in off the seas. Evidently Lake Ontario was going to keep the rest of the HOMER WARREN for herself.

Chief Kerr arrived at Oswego's North & Mitchell undertakers with Mr. Milnes and Coroner W.J. Nepham, and local investigators J.B. McMurrich and Captain Le Beau. All were present to identify remains and personal effects, and to attempt to form some impression about what happened to the WARREN. Both Chief Kerr and Mr. Milnes identified two of the sailors as the Kerr boys, and another as the captain's brother George Stalker. The final body was that of artist and cook, Patrick Howe. All bodies were badly bruised—mute evidence of a violent end.

Once the investigators were past the sorrowful task of body identification, they set themselves to solving the riddle of the WARREN's loss. The Bear Creek farmer's account of an unidentified lakeboat that was there and then gone with faint distress signals, had run in the Oswego Daily Palladium Wednesday evening and the investigators had the newspaper at hand. Another piece of the puzzle was a watch, worn by one of the sailors, that had stopped at 10 o'clock. Using that, along with the holed lifeboat, the marine men surmised that the WARREN, after departing Oswego, turned on her westward course and was making good time until the storm overtook her. Something happened then to put the boat at a disadvantage against the weather, and Captain Stalker was forced to turn and run before the winds toward the shelter of Sodus Bay, a shelter that he never reached.

In modern times we can look back across the decades and do some surmising of our own. Figuring time, speed and distance between the boat's departure and the stopped watch, as well as projecting the turn, and the farmer's sighting, the boat was making about six miles per hour or better "over the bottom speed." This was a healthy speed for a fully-loaded wooden lakeboat of the WARREN's class in good weather, let alone into the face of an October gale. If the storm was taking advantage of the WARREN, it was not doing so until shortly before the captain made his turn to run. Also, whatever happened allowed at least enough time for some of the crew to secure lifejackets around themselves. The logical scenario would have Captain Stalker driving the boat full ahead into the growing storm, when suddenly her 56 year old seams began to work and leak. His only option at that point would be to run for shelter. With things looking hopeless, her crew would have mustered to abandon ship, donned lifebelts and started the boats over the side. Since the WARREN's whistle was heard until about 10 o'clock (and that is the time that all evidence shows she went down) it is probable she had steam to the end, and thus would be flooded forward. Picked up by a following sea and down by the head, her cargo forced her forward and the HOMER WARREN took a nose-dive from beneath those struggling to abandon her. Bodies are pummeled, lifeboats beaten—and the whole matter is settled in seconds.

To say that this was exactly what happened to the WARREN and her people would be the ultimate in arrogance. Only those aboard her that morning know for sure what precisely transpired in the boat's final moments. As of this writing the shattered remains of the HOMER WARREN have yet to be found—and she is still lost somewhere in one of the deepest parts of Lake Ontario. As the technology for exploring the lakes grows more advanced and less expensive, boats such as the WARREN may be found. Normally these discoveries ask more questions than they answer.

On October 28th, 1919, a man known only as "Thompson" and another who will forever remain anonymous, were lost to Lake Ontario. In the days that followed the WARREN's loss, many a vesselman visited the Parsons store, some to buy an item or two or perhaps to send a wire, but most were there to see a painting that was on prominent display. It was a simple painting of the Oswego River, painted by a simple cook who shortly thereafter sailed to his doom aboard the HOMER WARREN—artist Patrick Howe. On May 14, 1940, John S. Parsons passed away and his collection of art was donated to the Oswego Historical Society. In the decades that followed, volunteer members of the Society fell into the casual habit of borrowing an item or two for display in their homes and businesses, normally returning the piece, but sometimes forgetting their obligation to preservation. In the 1960s this practice was halted and the Society's collection was finally secured. Today, among the hundreds of watercolors, oils and pictures, there are no images of the Oswego River signed by anyone named Howe. The artist's work, like Patrick Howe himself, has been lost. Perhaps like the two unknown crewmen, the painting is just unsigned and misplaced.

It is said that when an artist dies, his or her works become highly valuable. If that is so, then there is a work of great value and historical significance that could be just "floating" around out there someplace. If the readers of this story should find themselves in the eastern Lake Ontario area, they may want to look more carefully when cleaning that basement or attic, or when shopping at that consignment shop, Goodwill store, yard or estate sale—or perhaps in their own living room. Look for the 1919 painting signed by Patrick Howe, and bring it to the Oswego Historical Society. It is the last painting of his life and it may be, like the HOMER WARREN, out there somewhere . . . waiting to be found.

Trolling for History

Halfway up the thumb of Michigan, the view of Lake Huron seen from the beaches of Lexington, presents a glittering blue horizon of peace, on a fine summer day. The breath-taking splendor is marked from time to time by a lakeboat crawling along the distance on the upbound or downbound track. The whole scene resembles a postcard to the casual passerby, driving along route 25, with the spaces between the cottages presenting tantalizing sapphire glimpses of the lake. It is a peace that eternally and effectively disguises the resting place of many a lakeboat, the graves of many a drowned crewman, the forgotten stories of many a survivor. With a bit of imagination, the casual visitor to the Sanilac or Lexington shore may scan that blue distance and visualize the perils of vessels and crews, long since passed . . .

In modern times, research divers armed with high-tech tools, set out to uncover these lost adventures. Sometimes the task is easy, and sometimes it is confounding. Estimates of the number of wrecks that rest silently beneath the waters of the five Great Lakes range from 3,700 to more than 5,000—more than 1,300 wrecks have been misplaced in history's vortex. In many cases the historical records of a given vessel state simply "vessel lost," or "vessel burned," usually followed by just the year of the loss, and seldom with any location. Many proud lakers thus faded from existence, leaving no paper-trail whatsoever.

On the 28th day of June, 1988 the bulk of the membership of the Great Lakes Shipwreck Exploration Group shuffled into the Port Sanilac Bakery. Peering into the glass case that contained the trays of assorted doughnuts were research divers Jim Stayer, Garry Biniecki, Tim Juhl and Paul Rich. Their pointing fingers selected a solid day's supply of circular pastry, enough to sustain them through a lengthy day of wreck searching. The one member of the group missing was Jim's wife, Pat, busy teaching a swimming class. As the four men headed out of Port Sanilac and onto Lake Huron, doughnuts safely tucked away, they found themselves sailing into one of those postcard-perfect mornings. Their mission today was simple. They were out to christen the new side-scan sonar rig that Jim and Garry had acquired, and the ideal way to do that was to search for a virgin shipwreck.

Eyeing the number of wrecks that presented potential targets, each member had selected his favorite wreck. Garry persuaded the group that their best chance lay in finding the wreck of schooner-barge CHECOTAH. Lost on October 30, 1906 while in tow behind the steamer TEMPEST, the CHECOTAH had remained hidden beneath Lake Huron's waves, nearly forgotten for seven decades. The middle barge in a tow of three, downbound and lumber-laden, the CHECOTAH started losing the battle with the October gale that had swallowed it. As the CHECOTAH was becoming waterlogged, she was cut loose from the other boats. Rolling helplessly on the angry lake, the stricken schooner-barge neared her end, and the crew took to the yawl and abandoned her to the lake. An hour later, the castaways were picked up by the steamer WILLIAM A. PAYNE. No human saw the CHECOTAH go to the bottom. This story made the long-lost barge a ripe target for the Great Lakes Shipwreck Exploration Group.

To coordinate the search, Tim had set up two grids to be searched separately, one to the east and one to the west. It was felt that the long-lost CHECOTAH rested in the east grid, so the borderline between the grids was going to be used to calibrate and test the sonar equipment; then they would turn back and start the search. With a spicing of anticipation, the divers lowered the sonar fish over the side and started trolling for history. While Paul wheeled the boat and Jim watched the first penned lines on the graph strip, Tim and Garry broke out the doughnuts and coffee. Almost before the first mouthfuls could be swallowed, the pen suddenly spiked on the graph and scribbled a large object on the bottom of Lake Huron. "We have a target!" Jim bellowed. In less than one doughnut, the CHECOTAH had been found. She was just inside the west grid.

After the initial painting of the target, the search boat was turned and the wreck was graphed once more. On the second pass turn, a second anomaly scratched onto the graph tape, about 600 feet from the CHECOTAH. This seemed to be just a large hunk of wreckage that had been washed off the barge, and was quickly forgotten in the excitement over finding the main wreck. There was no way the divers could know that little spike anomaly would turn into a mystery that would puzzle them for over a year, and one of the most significant finds in the ice water museum. The jubilant divers decided to return to dry land to pick up Pat Stayer so that the whole group could come back and dive the wreck. By the time they all were once again hovering over the newly-found CHECOTAH, the weather had taken a drastic turn and rough seas prohibited diving. The schooner-barge would have to wait.

Throughout the summer of 1988 the group did manage to dive on the sunken CHECOTAH, photographing her hulk and documenting her wreckage. In order to protect the sleeping schooner-barge from marauding souvenir hunters, her identity and position had to be kept a closely-guarded secret. More than once the group headed out toward the CHECOTAH's grave, only to sight another boat in the area. Casually, they would turn away from the wreck's location and run off in a random direction to avoid suspicion. Twice, on doing this, the sonar graph showed that same phantom spike just off the CHECOTAH. Each time the anomaly appeared, it became more and more intriguing. Once the spike rose up so high that Paul Rich felt compelled to jot down the Loran coordinates.

The morning of August 12th, 1988 found Jim, Pat, Tim and Garry heading out once more for the CHECOTAH, and again, another boat was loitering uncomfortably close to the dive site, so the group decided to track over and investigate the phantom object. Sailing over to the Loran coordinates, they simply used their fish-finder to locate the object jutting 20 feet off the bottom. Jim dropped the anchor at a point he estimated to be near or over the highest point on the anomaly. Now among themselves, the divers had to decide who would go first. Garry gave up his turn, since he had already been down on a newly-discovered wreck, and this sonar spike was most likely the deck house from the CHECOTAH, not found on the wreck. With the toss of a coin, Jim was left on deck and Pat and Tim prepared to dive. The choice as to who would go and who would stay was not quite as casual as it appeared, for the bottom was just over 120 feet down, giving the divers about 12 minutes in the water, if they were to return without the need for decompression. This would be followed by a prudent four to six hour wait before diving again. Anyone who went down on this dubious object would probably sacrifice their dive on the CHECOTAH later in the day. As he wriggled into his dive gear Tim mumbled that he knew why the other two were letting him and Pat go first, "It's probably just a pile of lumber or somethin'" he quipped. Both divers went over the side and started down the line.

As she descended down the line, Pat Stayer felt as if it were taking a very long time to reach the bottom. Perhaps it was anticipation or excitement, but the seemingly long fall took only about a minute and a half, when a big circular shadow materialized in the darkness ahead and suddenly loomed into a giant black hole. Pat reached out and veered to avoid being swallowed by the opening. Pushing solidly off the lip of the big pipe-like breach, she descended further and came to rest in a jumble of massive machinery. For a long moment she was awe-struck, hip-deep in ancient machinery and facing a giant boiler. It was the opening where a smoke stack had been that had nearly swallowed Pat. Surrounded by wreckage, she looked over at Tim equally surprised. He gestured for her to look over her shoulder. Towering behind her stood nearly half of a giant wooden hogging arch.

It took only moments before the shock wore off, and the realization set in that the two divers were standing on the decks of an extremely old shipwreck. But the bottom time was rapidly running out, and the two divers must take full advantage of the few minutes remaining. With considerable haste, they moved toward the bow. The hull, except for the bow, was largely intact. The sides were collapsed, the decks were gone, and there were no deck houses or any other kind of accommodations visible. Before they could reach the bow, time ran out and the two headed back to the line. As they reached midships, Tim suddenly went over the side, having the thought that a boat this old might be a sidewheeler—but there were no buckets attached to the beams. What he did find was an old style porthole, which would turn out to be the only intact one on the boat.

On the surface, Jim and Garry waited patiently, and soon the bubbling signs of the divers return grew strong. Suddenly Tim burst from below and practically spit out his mouthpiece. "It's a steamer," he half-shouted and half-gasped "and it's got arches!" There followed a scene of jubilation, culminated with Garry springing from the dive-boat into a back flip. Plans to dive the CHECOTAH were forgotten as Jim and Garry scrambled with their gear and flopped into the lake. The odd spike on the sonar graph had turned out to be one of the Great Lakes long-lost shipwrecks. As the giddy divers motored back toward shore, they excitedly speculated on the identity of their newly found jewel. An arched steamer lost off Sanilac. "This one will be easy to identify," Tim said. These words he would not soon live down.

Unlike the excited divers heading back to Port Sanilac that day in 1988, we do not have to wait 14 months to solve the mystery of the long-lost arched steamer. The beginning of the story can be found by flipping the calendar back 1340 months, from the day the divers discovered the wreck. The Sanilac shore was a somewhat different place on October 12, 1876. Certainly the sky-blue lake would be there, but crawling along the horizon would be wooden schooners with soiled white canvas hoisted upon lofty masts, wooden steam-barges billowing clouds of thick black coal smoke from tall stacks, and gleaming white passenger and package propellers and sidewheelers. The port of Sanilac was nothing more than a gathering of houses, surrounded by farm land and reached far more easily by boat than by muddy road. On that same day Captain Michael Galvin could be found keeping a watchful eye on the loading of the lumber cargo into his charge, the propeller NEW YORK, moored to the Cove Island lumber dock at the mouth of Georgian Bay.

Loading of the NEW YORK was progressing, one plank at a time, handled by the boat's crew and the dock wallopers. Behind the steamer, waiting her to tow them, were the schooner-barges BUTCHER BOY, NELLIE McGILVRA and R.J. CARNEY, each preparing to carry their own burden. The drudgery of loading complete, Captain Galvin would guide the four boats from Cove Island and down Lake

Originally working as a passenger steamer, the NEW YORK was pressed into the lumber trade by 1874. With her cabins lopped off amidships, room was made for stacks of timber. No photos exist of her; this drawing is the author's concept.

Huron. The trip to Buffalo would take the better part of five days, but by 1876 standards that was akin to rapid transit.

Launched at Buffalo in September 12th of 1856, from the Buffalo Creek yard of shipbuilders Bidwell and Banta opposite Chicago Street, the NEW YORK was passed at once into the hands of her original owner, Stephen D. Caldwell of Dunkirk, New York. Captain C.H. Ludlow was given the honor of bringing out what was called "one of the finest steamers on the lakes." By any standard of the era, she was an elegant beauty, one of the more modest "palace steamers" that Bidwell and Banta had become famous for turning out. With her curved deck extending 182 feet from her bow to a bluntly rounded-stern, at a gross weight of 833 tons, the boat was a work of shipbuilding art. She was assigned an insurance rating of A2 and the inspectors placed a value of $28,500 on her. Captain Ludlow led the NEW YORK straight to work, running between Dunkirk and Toledo, a route on which she would spend most of her career.

In many ways, the NEW YORK was similar to others that were given birth in the late 1850s. Sideports opened into a reverberant cargo hold that could be stuffed with up to 600 tons of packaged cargo, and atop that were passenger accommodations rivaling the best hotels of the time. Normally the passenger rooms were aligned along a common passageway, with the entrance to each closed by a curtain, but in the NEW YORK the staterooms were divided by folding wooden doors, a true luxury. Each room was appointed with a bed, dresser and cistern to insure a first class passage. A long common dining room was located aft, topped with a cathedral-like skylight. Boats of this style were equipped with giant wooden arches attached to their beams, that were thought to stiffen the hull from "hogging." These vessels were by far the most efficient means of transporting persons and goods anyplace about the lakes. After all, this was the time when interstate highways were a century away, and the first mass-produced automobile was more than half of that into the future.

Unique to the NEW YORK's construction was her propulsion equipment. The steamer was outfitted with two oscillating engines of the Pin Crank type, with each engine driving a separate four-blade cloverleaf propeller. Such twin screw arrangements were rare on the lakes and oscillating steam engines were even more unusual. The popularity of twin screws did not become common on any lakeboat, until the rise of the 1000 footer in the late 1970s and early 1980s. Both engines were endowed with low pressure oscillating cylinders that measured 30 inches in diameter with a 30 inch stroke. The valves were patented by H.O. Perry, later to gain fame for designing the first successful compound steam engine for the maritime industry. No matter how she was viewed, the NEW YORK was a very special lakeboat.

In 1860 the NEW YORK changed ownership for the first time, moving to the hands of Nathaniel Marsh, receiver of the New York and Erie Rail Road and Steamboat Company, also of Dunkirk. Captain John Kirby was given command of the boat under this management, and she continued to run between Dunkirk and Toledo. In 1862 she was given a new master, Simon Moore, and although her owners remained the same, she, along with the rest of the fleet, was managed by Daniel Drew. Re-measured in 1865 at 184.8 feet in length, 29.4 feet in beam and 11.8 feet in depth, the NEW YORK remained a work horse of the fleet. She was given an insurance rating of B1, and her value was dropped to $26,000. No doubt the boat was beginning to show signs of age.

Over her years with the Erie Rail Road and Steam Boat Company, the NEW YORK went about her work fairly quietly, with one exception. On October 21st, 1859 she was involved in a collision with the schooner DAWN at Port Stanley, Ontario, resulting in the schooner sinking. Aside from that, the steamer sailed on for most of the next decade without a scrape. In the spring of 1868, she was given a new ceiling and decking at a cost of $6,000—in hopes of another routine and profitable season to come. This may have marked the end of the boat's quiet days. Her first bruise of the season came on the peaceful summer night of July 16th. Captain Hewett was bringing the NEW YORK out of Toledo, when he sighted the brig C.P. WILLIAMS making a course across his bow. Per regulation, the conscientious master ordered the NEW YORK checked down to a stop, to give way to the wind-grabber. The NEW YORK had come nearly to a halt, when the passing brig veered and crunched into her bow. Suffering from minor leaking and a shattered stem, the NEW YORK returned to Toledo for repairs—the WILLIAMS merely sailed away with a broken rail. Three months later, nearly to the day, on October 17th, Captain George W. Stoddard drove the NEW YORK onto a pier at Cleveland, damaging an arch and twisting some hull timbers. It was her last season under "E.R.R. St. Bt. Co." and it was not a good one.

On May 24th, 1869 she was merged into the Union Steamboat Company, as that parent company tightened the grip on its Erie Railroad subsidiary. Taking possession, they performed an extensive overhaul on the NEW YORK, as they invested money in freshening up all the boats in the Union fleet. It is unclear what exactly was done to the NEW YORK, but work done to others like her, caught in the same company movement, included new planking, re-calking, new frames and, sometimes, new arches. When she began running out of Dunkirk for the Union Steamboat interests, the NEW YORK's value was boosted to $28,000 once again, probably due to the overhaul.

With the start of the 1874 season, the Union Steamboat Company spent $10,000 to rebuild the NEW YORK for use in hauling lumber from the upper lakes. Again there is no record of exactly how she was converted, but it is reasonable to guess that her modification was similar to others of her class, such as her running mate the previous season, the PASSAIC. The deck house would be lopped off one cabin length behind the pilothouse, and cleared as far back as the galley bulkhead, save for the engine room skylight. The bird-cage pilothouse and hogging arches would be spared, along with her gangways, for her records show a tonnage reduction to 704 gross, consistent with this kind of conversion. The NEW YORK joined the booming lumber trade, as the ice began to clear in the spring of 1874, with a B2 insurance rating and estimated value of $16,000.

For only the second time in her long career, the little steamer was sold, this time to the McPherson family of Buffalo. A sum of $20,000 was what it cost to put the NEW YORK in their hands, just $4,000 more than her insured value. This, like the decision to convert her from the marginally-profitable passenger and package trade to the low overhead lumber business, was probably a result of the economic panic of 1873. The McPhersons assigned command of the steamer to Captain Michael J. Galvin, who would find his time aboard the NEW YORK more of an adventure than he had expected.

A blinding snowstorm had come early to eastern Lake Erie, and caught right in the midst of it was the NEW YORK, and Captain Galvin. With no aids to navigation except a compass and a clock, blinded by snow, the tiny laker ran straight into Point Abino, where the winds and waves began to take instant advantage of her. The date was November 3rd, 1874 and reports afterward used terms such as "total wreck," and "abandoned to the underwriters," to tell of her fate. Actually, she was recovered nine days later and taken to Buffalo for repairs. Captain Galvin brought her back out the following spring, and she returned to towing barges and hauling lumber as if the whole incident had never happened. For nearly another two full seasons, the NEW YORK worked quietly in the lumber trade—until October of 1876 brought her to Cove Island.

Not being a man who let superstition interfere with his command, Captain Galvin ordered the NEW YORK's lines cast off of the lumber dock on Friday the 13th day of

October, 1876. A cloud of white steam burst from the two foot tall soot-stained brass whistle, as the master blew a single blast to signal the NEW YORK leaving the dock. It was a sound that split the cold autumn air for miles, and echoed through the brilliant orange and yellow of the Canadian woods. The NEW YORK and her three lumber-laden schooner-barges were on their way down Lake Huron.

Dawn the following day was dark, gray and blowing a nasty fall storm. As the NEW YORK and her consorts pounded across Lake Huron, the water was no longer the postcard blue expanse. It was a boiling gray beast that humped its frigid back as if trying to throw the boats from its surface. From the north, northwest came a bitter shrieking wind, whipping the sea into a tempest. Early season snow squalls were mixed intermittently with the merciless wind. From the NEW YORK's pilothouse, Captain Galvin kept a sharp watch for the Michigan shore through the window panes. Time after time, the boat dipped her bow into the stone gray seas as the waves came to beat upon her quarter. At length, the dark silhouette of land appeared through the squalls, and as far as Captain Galvin could tell, he had brought the NEW YORK and her consorts just below Point aux Barques. This was a guess, based upon the only aid to navigation at the captain's disposal, his own instincts. The unhappy fact was that the four boats had been carried far south of that point, and were in truth just above Port Sanilac.

Suddenly, the roll of the NEW YORK's worn wooden deck felt clearly different under Captain Galvin's feet. Instinctively, he turned his attention to the barges and saw that the towing hawser to the BUTCHER BOY had parted. The three schooner-barges were being swept toward the open lake, and before his eyes were swallowed by the snow. Immediately, Captain Galvin began to plan how to recover the strays, but even before he could bring the NEW YORK around, word came from below that the boat was taking on water. The lake had finally found the limits of the NEW YORK's careworn hull.

Soon, the inrushing ice water was threatening the fires that kept the boat alive with steam, and the master's plans were rapidly changed from recovery of the barges to saving his vessel. Ordering the wheelsman to "bring her over on the right wheel," Captain Galvin pointed the NEW YORK directly at the thumb of Michigan, a dozen miles off.

There was just no chance that the arched steamer would ever reach the distant beach. The leak was massive, and shortly after the boat was turned, her fires were snuffed out—leaving her powerless. Caught at the disposal of the angry lake, the NEW YORK drifted with the wind. To the top of the tall mast a distress signal was hoisted, and the hearts of the crew brightened, for a steamer with a tow of two schooner-barges appeared in the distance. Their hopes were dashed, however, at half past 11 that morning, when the three boats clawed past them on the storm-churned horizon. It was all too clear that the NEW YORK was on her way to Lake Huron's bottom, and Captain Galvin ordered the crew into the yawl boat—all 16 members of the crew went over the rail. At ten minutes before noon they caught the last sight of the steamer for 112 years, plunging to its permanent resting place beneath the white-caps. The survivors were now cramped into a tiny wooden lifeboat, tossed by the seas like a chip, and besieged by a frigid wind determined to push them out into the open lake. Water up nearly to their knees quickly numbed their feet as they bailed for their lives . . . waiting for whatever Lake Huron had in store.

A century and a dozen years later, the Great Lakes Shipwreck Exploration Group passed much of the winter of 1988 sifting through the information that might help them identify the wreck with the arches. Eventually Pat would complete a clay sculpture and archaeological drawing of the wreck, as it rests on the bottom. When research of the wreck began, the listings of more than 250 lakers lost on Lake Huron had to be considered, including the boats that had been seen sailing onto the lake, but never made port. There were the boats left in the open lake by their abandoning crew, listed simply as "last seen . . . " Finally there were the vessels that were mis-recorded in the historical documents, or had no record of their existence at all. Through paper shuffling alone, the list was trimmed to about a dozen possibilities. That is where the easy part ended.

Initially, the team had speculated that they might have found the EAST SAGINAW. This boat was about the right size, and it was always felt that the steamer had arches when she was lost. Perhaps she had drifted 23 miles south of where she had last been seen. Stranger things have happened on the lakes. The twin screws on the wreck eliminated this possibility, as it was supposed the EAST SAGINAW was a single screw boat. On one of the late fall dives, Garry had found a shattered steam gauge with "NEW YORK STEAM GAUGE CO. DAVIS PATENT, JULY 2, 1867," written on it. This narrowed the list, by eliminating any vessel lost before that date.

As the diving season opened in 1989, gauges with patent dates of 1854 were found, and if these were assumed to be original equipment, they narrowed the construction date. Later in the year a dinner platter, a hand cart, a capstan and steam whistle were found. Usually any of these could have had the boat's name or vessel line scribed upon them, but those from the mystery wreck did not. Through the process of elimination, the research divers had narrowed the list to just one vessel, the NEW YORK, but had no final proof. On the advice of John Stine at the Smithsonian, the group contacted Pat Labadie, director of the Canal Park Museum at Duluth, Minnesota. He forwarded rare information on the NEW YORK engine and boilers that matched the measurements and observations that the group had made, but absolute proof of the wreck's identity was yet to be secured. On October 8th, 1989 Tim and Pat were down on the wreck for the first time that day, when suddenly Tim heard Pat shout his name through the water. Thinking she was in trouble, Tim swam quickly to her and found the astonished diver pointing toward the last piece of the puzzle. As she had maneuvered her bright video lamp across the engine works, a golden glint reflected from the brackish muddle that all the divers had passed over many times. Through the swirling silt on one of the valves was a small brass plate inscribed "H.O. Perry patent, March 25th, 1856." It was one of the precise specifications that Mr. Labadie had listed in the NEW YORK's records. The long-forgotten wreck bore a name . . . at last.

Nearly five hours after the NEW YORK plummeted through 100 feet of Lake Huron on that stormy day in October of 1876 and slammed into the bottom, the giant cloud of silt raised by the impact had barely settled around the collapsed wreck. High over head, bobbing on the storm-raked surface, Captain Galvin and 15 of his crew were being brutalized by the gale. Even though huddled together for warmth, they were about to succumb to exposure. Just when things looked hopeless, a small schooner appeared on the horizon. It was the schooner NEMESIS, and her crew of three. She was hauling a cargo of tan-bark, under the command of Captain Spence of Southampton.

With all the strength they had left, the castaways waved and shouted. Onboard the NEMESIS, keen eyes spotted the crowded yawl, and all aboard the schooner knew just what must be done. Maneuvering as best she could, the little schooner pressed down on the lifeboat, but the storm pushed her way out of position, and she passed some distance off the yawl. Now Captain Spence would have to turn his sailing vessel back into the storm, tach above the yawl, turn again and make another pass. This would be a difficult, and some may say, impossible maneuver. The crew of three would have to scurry like mad ants, resetting lines and canvas. As the schooner came around, the seas reared up and bit away a large portion of her deck-load. Spearing her jib into the heaving waves, the NEMESIS careened into the wind—and after what seemed like a lifetime—made her second pass at the yawl. Again the waves and winds got the better of the wind-grabber.

In all, the NEMESIS made an incredible 12 battered passes before her beam finally scraped the yawl. Benumbed hands from each craft grasped one another, as the survivors were plucked from the lake's clutch. Unfortunately as William Sparks, one of the NEW YORK's firemen, was being pulled to safety he slipped and, in his weakened state, was instantly taken by the icy waters. The survivors were given what limited accommodations the NEMESIS could offer, and recovered rapidly from the ordeal. Around midnight, the rescue schooner rolled into Port Huron, minus most of her deck cargo, but proudly bearing 15 grateful souls. At about that same time, an odd arrangement of vessels sailed in off the angry lake. When she broke free of the NEW YORK, the BUTCHER BOY, first in the string of barges, hoisted her sails and towed the McGILVRA and CARNEY into port.

Today, the NEW YORK is protected as part of the Sanilac Shores Underwater Preserve. But those who found and documented the wreck were in fear that the scourge of the lakes, the souvenir hunter, might risk a felony charge

The NEW YORK as she appears on the bottom of Lake Huron, is a far cry from her proud days as an elegant passenger carrier. This drawing is by Pat Stayer, one of the research divers who discovered the forgotten wreck.

and steal some of her removable artifacts. Mindful of this Tim Juhl, representing the Sanilac Shores Underwater Preserve Committee, petitioned the State of Michigan for removal and preservation of the boat's steam whistle. Tim then had to defend the request before the State Underwater Preserve and Marine Salvage Committee, but at length, removal of the whistle was granted. As of this writing, the whistle is safe in the possession of the Great Lakes Shipwreck Exploration Group. Plans are to display it at the Sanilac County Historical Society, and later at the group's own information center. A steam generator will be attached to the whistle, and for the first time in over 100 years, the sound of the steamer NEW YORK will split the air and echo over the lake . . . and the countryside.

Trip 29

For the better part of a full day and night, the two marine legs from Buffalo, New York's Standard Grain dock's elevators have been stretched into the open hatches of the Interlake Steamship Company's 647 foot steamer J.L. MAUTHE. Hungrily, the belted clamshells that run the length of each leg, are chewing away at the boat's cargo of grain. Normally, this system could devour about 13,000 bushels per hour, but today the apparatus is running a bit slow at about 9,000 bushels per hour. It is dawn on Saturday, the fifth day of December, 1992 and the MAUTHE and her crew are engaged in the annual tradition of hauling as much late-season grain as possible from the upper lakes, before Arctic winds turn the freshwater seas to solid ice.

Buffalo has long been one of the major grain terminals on the Great Lakes, much longer than most people would think. The first trickles of grain came into the port just before 1830, within the next six years the business boomed, fed by the expanding farmlands to the west. By 1841 Buffalo harbor was a veritable forest of masts, attached to sailing vessels that had come east burdened with grain. The difficulty was the unloading method of the day, slow enough to make a snail's crawl appear swift. Block and tackle were used to lower baskets through the boat hatches, where the grain was shoveled in by hand and hoisted to a 10 to 15 bushel hopper and scale, suspended above. Weighed, it was bagged or barreled and carried ashore by immigrant laborers. To complicate this process, work must be halted each time rain fell or storm winds kicked up. Only 1,800 to 2,000 bushels could go ashore in a full day. At that rate, in modern times, it would take 345 days to unload one cargo carried by the MAUTHE.

Fortunately for the crew of the MAUTHE as well as the Interlake Steamship Company, a Buffalo businessman named Joseph Dart had a better idea in 1841. Borrowing a Revolutionary War era concept for milling grain developed by Oliver Evans called the "hopper-boy," Dart attached two-quart capacity buckets 28 inches apart on a continuous leather belt. The whole rig was attached to a long leg that could be extended directly from the elevator to a boat's cargo hold. A steam engine ran the whole contraption. Many around Buffalo scoffed at the device—after all, "Irishmen's backs," according to Dart's close friend Mahlon Kingsman, "are the cheapest elevators ever built." The critics were abruptly silenced when the schooner JOHN S. SKINNER, with 4,000 bushels aboard, was unloaded in just four hours proving Dart's belt-and-buckets were a marvel. Later, the buckets were enlarged and spaced closer on the belt. Additionally Longshoremen, or "scoopers," wielding giant wooden dustpan-like trays propelled by ropes driven off of the legs, were used to pile the tail ends of cargos at the buckets. By the 1860s, capacity was up to 7,000 bushels per hour. In the afternoon of December 5th, 1992, swirling snow squalls, mixed with grain dust, surround the J.L. MAUTHE as "scoopers" sling the last of her cargo toward the legs. No one remembers Joseph Dart, who invented the unloading gear they are using—which shortens the big steamer's dock time by 11 and one-half months—and put thousands of immigrants out of work.

Throughout the MAUTHE's unloading, an early winter gale had been sweeping across Lake Erie and dumping lake-effect snow from the Buffalo shore inland. Shuffling about in the pilothouse as the last grain went up the legs, is relief master, Captain Bryon "easy does it" Petz.

D.J. STORY PHOTO

Downbound into the St. Clair River, the J.L. MAUTHE appears here in the spring of 1993. Working her way through the season she will inevitably come to grip with another winter of grain haulin'.

Perusing the latest weather-fax, Captain Petz figures that the slightly lower rate of the unloading rigs will work in the MAUTHE's favor. The gales would be diminishing through the day, and the evening winds should turn to a bluster. Lake Erie, the shallowest of the Great Lakes, has a distinct tendency to become quickly enraged at the first taste of storm winds, but to die down just as rapidly when the winds subside. The MAUTHE's delay in unloading ought to allow just enough time for the lake to settle down.

As the scoopers finished their dusty toil, the MAUTHE's captain has two concerns on his mind that carry a far greater urgency than temperamental Lake Erie. A second storm system is, at the moment, upsetting Lake Superior. "There's a low passin' Superior at 29 even . . . " the captain informs Third Mate Doug Cooley, who is climbing the stairs to the pilothouse. The master's reference is to the barometric pressure being measured at 29.00 inches of mercury. 29.92 is considered standard, and the lower the pressure the stronger the storm. " . . . the lowest I ever saw it was 28.80," the master continues, with his attention drawn out across the MAUTHE's stern. Directly behind the steamer is the brooding black iron girders of the Ohio Street aerial lift bridge. It is the gateway to the tightest, and by all considerations, the worst, turn on the Great Lakes. Gales and ice the lake mariners take in stride, but the Ohio Street turn has kept many a captain awake at night. When the MAUTHE is empty, Captain Petz must back his boat through Ohio Street, with the aid of a single tug.

While the Dart marine legs are lifted from the now-empty hold, deckhands secure the last of the MAUTHE's giant steel hatch covers. Each hatch cover is a single plate, held in place by a series of clamps. Movement of the hatch covers requires the use of a deck-mounted crane, running the length of the spar deck on rails. Use of this "iron deckhand" makes placing the hatches a two-man job, at best. The last clamp snapped in place, the "G" tug IOWA hovers near the stern and lines are passed. In the pilothouse comes a pop and a hiss as the captain fires up the bow thruster. "Don't let this powerful thing throw ya' off your feet now," he quips to the wheelsman. The MAUTHE's bow thruster is a bit underpowered, and keeps captains on their toes especially at Ohio Street.

Like watching a clock run, the process of wiggling a 647 foot steamer through Ohio Street is worse than slow. With only a bit of ballast in her forward tanks to keep the bow thruster effective, the MAUTHE is slightly head down but riding about as high out of the water as she can. "We don't want any wind now," the master murmurs as the bow comes clear of the dock and the bridge begins to lift. On deck all three mates call out distances, in a team effort to overcome Ohio Street. Over channel 10 the first mate's voice crackles, " . . . closest point on the port quarter is about 36 feet," followed by the third mate's call from the bow, "36 feet off the wall, 36." The radio chatter reverberates through the pilothouse, the bridge footings vanish from view below the bow rail, and the captain and wheelsman must rely on the third mate, leaning over the side, to be their eyes. "Eight feet off these pilings on the fore-bow!" he calls, and after a long silence, "10 feet off the fore-bow," is transmitted in a more subdued tone. "That's it Doug, just keep talkin'," answers the captain. From deep below, the bow thruster rumbles and aft the tug IOWA zigzags with the towline. The Ohio Street pavement stretches out toward the hull, "and we're reachin' out toward the center of the next stretch," the first mate finally calls from astern, "you got daylight on that starboard side," comes from the bow. "Call 'em and tell 'em put 20 feet in two through six and let me know when it's in, Tom," the captain directs the wheelsman. The MAUTHE is clear of the bridge and needed ballast can now be pumped aboard. "20 feet two through six," the wheelsman echoes, cranking the bell on the engine room phone. The J.L. MAUTHE and crew have defeated Ohio Street again.

Interestingly, the crew of the MAUTHE make this turn with regularity, completely unaware of the melee that occurred there the night of January 21, 1959. It is a story that may just make them regard the Ohio Street turn in a different light. On that bitter Thursday night in 1959, the Kinsman Transit Company's 440 foot steamer Mac GILVRAY SHIRAS was sleeping in winter lay-up at the Concrete-Central Elevator at the upper end of Buffalo Creek. Downstream from the SHIRAS a dozen lakers also were hibernating at winter quarters along the river bank. This fleet included the 545 foot steamer MICHAEL K. TEWKSBURY, moored at the Standard Elevator from which the MAUTHE would take cargos 33 years later. With a gale blowing and ice floes wedged against her hull, the SHIRAS began parting her mooring lines just after 10 o'clock in the evening, and by 10:40 her massive hull was drifting downstream, driven by the wind. There was no crew manning the SHIRAS, just her flustered ship-keeper aboard. In an effort to stop the SHIRAS' drift, the ship-keeper released the anchors. Unfortunately, he had neglected to clear the "devil's claws" (used to keep the anchors from accidentally dropping), so the big chains became hopelessly jammed.

Miraculously, the SHIRAS drifted right down the center of the stream, sliding cleanly past every boat until she reached the Standard Elevator and the MICHAEL K. TEWKSBURY. As the SHIRAS rounded the bend above the Standard Elevator, she could not fit between the TEWKSBURY and the B.W. DRUCKENMILLER, in lay-up across the river. With a loud thump, the SHIRAS slammed stern-first into the TEWKSBURY's bow, forcing that boat to part her lines and similarly go adrift. At that moment, the two wayward lakeboats proceeded to do the impossible, together. Without aid of tugs, or rudders, or engine power, or even crews—they slipped through Ohio Street, made the turn and continued downstream. The entire rampage ended 37 minutes after it began, when the boats piled into the Michigan Avenue bridge. If the crew of the MAUTHE knew of this remarkable event, they would doubtless regard their present chore in a slightly different way.

After nearly two hours, the MAUTHE is clear of Buffalo Creek, poised behind the breakwater. The tug IOWA is set free, and using a hard-over rudder and the bow thruster the big steamer is pivoted nearly 180 degrees to point toward an ink-black Lake Erie. The chadburn rings to full ahead, and the captain calls down to the engine room to order the lake-gate. Distancing from the breakwater, the MAUTHE begins her familiar wobble, caused by one slightly-dinged propeller blade. The steering apparatus is set to "auto," and the superb steel steamer heads toward Long Point.

The auto-pilot is holding the wheel, but that by no means implies the pilothouse is vacated. A watch is kept from the windows constantly, for while the boat is moving, barely a second passes that at least one pair of eyes is not scrutinizing the distance, and both the MAUTHE radars keep an unending watch, beyond the point that the human eye can see. All that is visible in the distance this night is a single dim light on the far horizon ahead. The radar reveals a target, but the MAUTHE is closing at a rate of less than one mile each hour, so it will be dawn before the other upbounder will be close enough to deal with. Lake Erie has calmed to a dead swell. The captain turns the pilothouse over to the third mate as the MAUTHE steams into the night and the lights of Buffalo begin to fade astern. Trip number 29 has begun.

The big steamer is the smallest member of the immaculate fleet of lakeboats that comprise the Interlake Steamship Company. In an era that has seen many once-powerful U.S. Great Lakes fleets fade into history, or become a small division of some distant corporation, the historic Interlake fleet has stood against the hard times, enduring as the lakes themselves. While other fleets appear on the edge, Interlake sports four 1000 footers, or "footers" as the mariners call them. Formed in 1913, the company today has 11 bottoms with a combined single-trip carrying capacity of 389,567 tons. Interestingly, the 1948 Ship Masters Association Directory lists Interlake's single-trip fleet capacity at 364,900 tons, but that is using 36 vessels. Much has changed over the years, but one characteristic remains the same—Interlake has the character of a small local business where everyone, from deck-hand to executive, is as down-to-earth friendly as the corner shopkeeper of 1948.

When she came out of the Great Lakes Engineering Works River Rouge yard in 1953, the J.L. MAUTHE was hull number 298. Measuring 70 feet across her beam and 36 feet in depth, the MAUTHE was one of a half dozen nearly identical oreboats. The six boats were dubbed the "Pittsburgh class," since half of them, the ARTHUR M. ANDERSON, CASON J. CALLAWAY and PHILIP R. CLARKE, had gone to the once dominant Pittsburgh Steamship Company. The remaining boats, WILLIAM CLAY FORD and RESERVE, went to the Ford Motor Company and the Columbia Transportation Company, respectively. One trait set the MAUTHE apart to the casual boat watcher—the after cabins were one deck house shy of her sisters, giving her a slightly submarine-decker appearance.

A colorful December sunrise cracked through the clouds, long enough to brighten the MAUTHE's pilothouse, as she beat her way across Lake Erie near the Southeast Shoal light. About three miles ahead, the saltie LAKE TAHOE turned out to be the light the MAUTHE had been closing on through the night. As the two boats came into the zigzag channel that is Pelee Passage, the MAUTHE took her place in the saltie's wake for the trip up the Detroit and St. Clair rivers, while ahead, some downbounders are tracking through that same channel. It is a real bottleneck.

In the distance to the south, the tin-stacker CASON J. CALLAWAY pushes over the horizon and within the hour slides in line, upbound, three miles behind the MAUTHE. The marching order for the passage up appears to be the LAKE TAHOE, the J.L. MAUTHE and the CASON J. CALLAWAY, all with scarcely three miles between them.

Some seven miles below the Detroit River light, the MAUTHE is hauled around into the channel that will bring her into the lower Detroit River. At the same time the CALLAWAY appears to depart her course and angle away on a sharp northwest track. The MAUTHE's pilothouse binoculars show the CALLAWAY taking spray over her bow-rail and down her fence, while the MAUTHE has taken none at all. What is going on becomes clear: the CALLAWAY is cutting the corner running the shallows to buoys 13 and 14 in an effort to cut in front of the MAUTHE, already in the channel. In the MAUTHE's pilothouse, the consensus is that the CALLAWAY is set on taking fuel at the Shell dock in Sarnia, and by cutting in front of the MAUTHE, she can save the two hours for the Interlake boat to fuel. This may seem like a matter of little concern, but when you calculate the near $1,000 per hour cost of running a big laker, it is a gamble that some are willing to take. There is one hitch. The geometry will not work this time, and all that has been accomplished is that the CALLAWAY is now on a collision course with the MAUTHE.

With the MAUTHE running her course, the tin-stacker bores closer at about a 45 degree angle to the MAUTHE's beam and less than 300 yards away, so the Interlake boat has been forced into a real dilemma. If Captain Petz checks the MAUTHE's speed and at the same time the CALLAWAY realizes the futility of its short-cut and tucks in astern, the big self-unloader will run up the Interlake boat's fantail. On the other hand, with the MAUTHE running on the lake-gate, she has about as much speed as she can muster. If the CALLAWAY does manage to squeeze in ahead, when she turns onto the channel course she will lose forward way, and the MAUTHE will be forced into some heavy backing to avoid hitting her. Furthermore, if the CALLAWAY's steering equipment should fail now, she will most certainly ram the MAUTHE broadside, perhaps sending both boats to the bottom. All that the MAUTHE's crew can do is squeeze as far into the downbound lane as possible, and stand watching as the 767 foot CASON J. CALLAWAY charges directly at them.

Angling between the buoy and the MAUTHE, the CALLAWAY draws to within a few hundred feet of the Interlake oreboat. With a boat width between the vessels, the CALLAWAY enters the channel, hauling hard over, churning mud from the lake bottom. Deciding he wants no part of this, the MAUTHE's master rings to check the boat's speed—but the laws of physics are not easily cheated. The flow of water between the two massive hulls has created a venturi effect, and the MAUTHE is being pulled along with the tin-stacker. The captain rings down for 70 turns on the MAUTHE's big screw, and gradually the CALLAWAY slowly pulls ahead. "This ain't the place to be racin'," the captain rumbles to the wheelsman, "he wants it, let 'em have it." The master will take third in line, and a delay at the fuel dock, if it means finishing the trip safely.

Navigating the Detroit and St. Clair rivers, like all of the connecting waterways on the Great Lakes, is a unique process. Proper charts are pulled from their drawer and laid out on the table, but rarely used. The mariners who peer from the center windows of lakeboats, if they are third, second or first mates, or captains, know these waterways so well that the turns, headings and landmarks are ingrained in their souls. Today the MAUTHE will be brought up the lower Detroit River by Second Mate Jeff Green, a veteran of the lakes since 1967, and at the end of his fourth season on the MAUTHE. Standing at the wheel behind the mate is wheelsman Gary Myjak, who started on the lakes in 1966 and has steadied the MAUTHE's wheel for 17 years. To say these mariners are experienced would be an understatement in the extreme.

"Just left her easy to that smokestack, that tall one with the smoke comin' out there," the mate directs casually, and Myjak nimbly manipulates the wheel, as if the boat were a part of him. That is how it is done. Just as a good chess player can call moves from across the room because the whole board is pictured in his mind, the lake mariner calls each turn with the whole river pictured in his mind. Not only is the proper landmark important, but the speed that the point of the steering pole appears to move from one landmark to another, is essential. The mariner can discern when a turn is coming around too slow or too fast, whereas an untrained observer can see no difference. "Now bring her onto that apartment building and that should give you 74," the mate continues. "On the apartment building . . . " the wheelsman echoes, as the compass repeater clicks to 074 degrees, " . . . 74." Selected at the right spot, the proper landmark gives the right heading. Even the rate that the wheelsman hears the repeater click is used in judging the turns.

In the MAUTHE's pilothouse, as the boat glides up the river, is Deck-Cadet Richard Ruth from the Great Lakes Maritime Academy. As part of their training, the cadets must sail 350 days, using multiple vessels of various fleets. Today, Richard has a neatly detailed and intricately hand-drawn chart of the Detroit and St. Clair rivers spread out in the chart room. His job is the seemingly impossible task of learning the rivers, while being taught and quizzed by the pilothouse crew. All around the boat, the cadet will repeat the process with all of the crew. For Richard, the MAUTHE is a floating, hands-on classroom, open around the clock.

The Ambassador Bridge looms ahead, as the mail-boat J.W. WESTCOTT II angles out to the MAUTHE. The little boat is a lifeline providing much more than mail, since the freighters it serves never have to stop. Today the delivery consists of mail for the crew, some company items, a stack of Sunday papers and one special package, a center-piece arrangement of flowers from "the flower lady." There are numerous stories as to why the flower lady sends arrangements to various boats as they pass, but the fact remains

D.J. STORY PHOTO

Sulking at the lock wall on June 26, 1993, the CASON J. CALLAWAY shows no regrets at having once conflicted with the J.L. MAUTHE. In an industry where hours value in thousands of dollars, such conflicts are a part of the business.

that Arlene Earl sends the arrangements—and expects only a whistle salute in return. Passing Harsens Island, the master seizes the whistle-pull and sounds one long and two shorts, steps out onto the bridge-wing and gives a grateful wave as they pass the flower lady's house.

Darkness has fallen as the MAUTHE approaches Stag Island and the captain checks the speed to a snail's crawl. Currently the CALLAWAY is squatting at the Shell Oil fuel dock, just above the island, and the MAUTHE must hold back for the tin-stacker to clear. Shortly the CALLAWAY calls the Interlake boat, and advises that about 10 more minutes will be needed—as promised, the dock is clear in a half hour and the MAUTHE eases up and makes her lines secure. A giant hose is put over the side, and the dock proceeds to pump aboard 72,197 gallons of bunker-C diesel oil. The tanks can handle 149,000 gallons, but at an average consumption of 11,500 gallons per day, a substantial portion of what she is now taking aboard will be burned before she reaches the grain dock at Superior. In just over an hour the hose is back aboard, and the steamer is headed through what remains of the St. Clair River and on to Lake Huron, as the 730 foot ALGOSOUND takes her place at the dock.

As hazardous as it is, late-season navigation does eliminate one menace from the lake mariner's job, for which they are eternally grateful—and that is the careless pleasure-boater. During pleasant weather the Detroit and St. Clair rivers are swarming with pleasure craft, most going about their leisure with careful consideration, but there are a few seeming to want a bit more. Unfortunately this often involves an elaborate game of dodging across the path of an oncoming lake freighter. With no consideration for the inability of a laker to stop suddenly, or turn with any kind of urgency, these weekend sailors will turn their egg-shell frail fiberglass boats, and cut directly in front of a passing steel monster lakeboat. The laker crew can only hold their collective breath, to see if the pleasure boat that disappeared from view comes again into sight. A big laker could easily crush a pleasure boat, and the freighter's crew would never feel the impact. Most of the time the careless boaters emerge, shouting and laughing as if they have won some game. Onboard the MAUTHE they tell the tale of another laker, from which a pleasure craft did not reappear. When the oreboat crew dashed to the rail expecting to find people in the water, they found the pleasure craft up along side—with its occupants spray-painting graffiti on the freighter's beam! Clearly such incidents are rare and not all pleasure boaters are reckless, but there are enough to make the lakeboat crews appreciate the onset of foul weather, especially where the St. Clair River meets Lake Huron.

Into the blackness of Lake Huron the MAUTHE churns. It is after midnight, and a noticeable quiet fills the boat. Of course there is unending vigilance in the pilothouse, and a constant watch in the engine room, but the crew not on duty are taking advantage of a rare commodity, the privacy of their rooms. Those on duty are performing the tedious painting and stowing tasks, common to a freighter, in various locations around the boat. Walking around the boat at this time of night, one could get the impression of being on some ghost ship. In the windlass room every item is in its place and only the sound of the waves pounding the bow breaks the stillness. A deck below, the washer and dryer and the crew's exercise equipment await use. Onboard boats of the MAUTHE's class, one can pass from bow to stern by one of two tunnels, running along the boat's beam just below the spar deck. The tunnel is empty, too, and filled only by the loud noise of large fans, circulating overheated air. Astern, the scene is much the same as forward, except for more noise and vibration.

Galley accommodations on the MAUTHE are in the stern, and in the wee hours of the night, they too are vacant. Hanging pots and pans clang together and dinner left-overs are kept warm in big foil-covered pans. Crew members who feel like a late night snack can help themselves, or explore the big refrigerator for sandwich material. Three meals each day are served aboard the MAUTHE, with the second cook serving the officer's dining room, the porter serving the crew's eating area and the cook reigning over the whole domain. Oddly, the galley is the one place on a lakeboat where the most formality can be sensed. On the MAUTHE, seats are assigned at the officer's table by the second cook, and plates are carefully set down in front of you—no need to reach up. The daily menu is listed on an erasable board and every meal is "all you can eat." The MAUTHE's cook and galley czar Don Cook sees to that.

Meals onboard the MAUTHE are served on a schedule the crew know by heart. Supper is served from half past four o'clock in the afternoon until half past five and includes two kinds of meat, and enough vegetables and trimmings to stuff the hungriest crewman. Lunch is a combination of breakfast items, for crew whose duties will not allow them to make that meal, and mid-day sandwiches, burgers and salads, all served in the hour before noon. From 7:30 a.m. until 8:30 a.m. breakfast is presented and offers every selection and combination imaginable, including the finest blueberry pancakes on the planet. Crewmembers never really crowd the galley, they simply drift in at their convenience and leave well-fed. Meals are the opportunity for the crew to exchange the latest gossip too, keeping with the tradition of the galley as the universal exchange point for unofficial ship's news.

Beating her way northward the MAUTHE begins to face a continually stiffening wind. As the boat comes abeam Point aux Barques on the tip of Michigan's thumb, the winds are gusting to 40 miles per hour and gale warnings are up for Lake Huron. Meeting the eight to 12 foot seas nearly head-on, the big steamer is beginning to take spray over the rail. Her bluff bow pounds from time to time making a low "boom" sound, like the slamming of a distant warehouse door . . . the lake mariners say she's "stubbin' her toe." Spray is no problem, but the one thing the captain does not like to do is roll the boat, and once the MAUTHE clears the thumb, the west wind will put seas on her beam and she will roll. Just above the point, the boat is hauled around to the west and runs across the mouth of Saginaw Bay. To take advantage of the lee of land, the MAUTHE is tucked up against the Michigan shore once more.

At dawn the winds are still blowing strong, at times strengthening to 40 miles per hour and lingering there. Still hugging the Michigan shore, the MAUTHE is coming upon Alpena. A streak of black smoke comes from the shoreline, and the S.T. CRAPO, one of the last coal-burners, comes into binocular range. She is downbound for Alpena and hugging even closer to the coast. A single wave slaps the MAUTHE's bow and throws a drenching spray onto the pilothouse windows, where it promptly freezes. This is December navigation.

Late afternoon on December 7th finds the snow whitened gap of Detour Passage greeting the big Interlake steamer. As forecast, the winds have faded to a gusty bluster, and from the MAUTHE's pilothouse the Coast Guard buoy tender BUCKTHORN is seen, lifting buoys from the Saint Marys River before the winter ice can crush them. Down in the MAUTHE's windlass room the anchors are being "cleared." This work is performed before the boat goes into any river, and involves removal of the equipment that prevents anchors from accidentally dropping. First the "devil's claws," two steel hooks supported by cables, are removed. These flat steel catches are hooked through a link in each of the anchor chains, and should the equipment holding the chain slip, they are designed to keep the anchors aboard. Next, the wing-nuts holding down the steel plates covering the hawsepipes are removed and the plates lifted. The hawsepipe is the opening through which the anchor chain passes when let go and, although the MAUTHE's are nearly a dozen feet long, the lake will often shoot up them in a rough sea. Supposedly, the covers are to keep the intruding water out, but such is not the case. Old pillows are stuffed beneath the plates aboard the MAUTHE to block the lake and are, in fact, quite effective. When upbound, only the forward anchors need to be cleared, but downbound the stern anchor is also cleared. With her hooks free, the MAUTHE pushes toward the Soo.

Like a sleeping Christmas display, the city of Sault Saint Marie slides past the MAUTHE, and with surgical care the crew lines the boat up, easing her toward the MacArthur lock. As the bow comes "up against," a crewman is swung over the side on the boom and the moment it can be swung back, a second crewman is sent over. Lines from the boat are passed to hands on the pier and the MAUTHE moves into the lock. The whole scene resembles a cross between a long-running Broadway play and some sort of circus act. It is fascinating to spectators, but those who are performing have done it so many times, they barely give their work a second thought. With the chadburn ringing and the radio squawking, the MAUTHE eases into the confines of the lock and the lower gates close behind. In less than an hour the process is complete, and the steamer is headed toward open Lake Superior once more.

Steadily widening, the Saint Marys River opens into Whitefish Bay and, with the Lake Superior temper well in mind, the captain retires for the night. The winds on this largest lake are out of the west and again reaching 40 miles per hour, but the waves are forming only a large dead swell. "If that wind shifts north come down and get me"—the master's orders are unusually dour in tone—"I mean if it even starts swingin' anywhere near toward the north. I don't want it comin' at us like that while it's in the fourth notch." Lake Superior is never to be trifled with and a more northerly wind could set the MAUTHE rolling in a beam sea. The "fourth notch" is slang that refers to the mayfor code attached to wind velocity in knots with 0 being 0-10, 1 being 11-16, 2 being 17-21, 3 being 22-27, 4 being 28-33, 5 being 34-40, 6 being 41-47, 7 being 48-55, 8 being 56-63 and 9 being over 63. Late-season navigation demands constant vigilance, for a slight shift in the winds can lead to a howling gale.

Awaking with the first light of December 8th, the crew on the MAUTHE can feel the deck barely moving beneath their feet. It would seem the boat is in shelter, but a quick glance from the port hole shows the steamer underway, and making good time. The forecast gale has disintegrated and the boat is in the middle of the pleasant side of late-season sailing. Under calm sky and on top a nearly flat sea, the steamer churns through the day toward the head of the lakes.

At 90 turns of her giant propeller, the immense steamer produces 7000 horsepower and can make upwards of 15 miles per hour. The steam turbine engine, that pulses like a heart deep in her stern, sports a complex array of hissing pipes and gauges that distracts from the simplicity of the engine's basic operation. Water is drawn from the lake at a spot two miles above Whitefish Point, or if running lower lakes routes, above Lake Michigan's Bone Reef, where the best is found and purified through condensers. The immaculate water is fed to the boilers and turned into steam. (It is interesting that the potable water used for drinking and cooking is taken at the same spots and used without purification, while the boiler's water must be far cleaner than the human's water.) Steam is next passed over a turbine, and through the use of reduction gearing they turn the screw. Although the nuts and bolts of every system is complex, the basic function is this simple. All of this in no way makes Chief Liimatta and his staff's job a simple matter. They not only keep the original equipment of the MAUTHE's engine workings moving smoothly, but they are responsible for everything else on the boat, from a leaky sink to a stubborn winch.

Three miles away from the Duluth canal, the MAUTHE radios the famous aerial lift bridge that spans the waterway. The bridge tender has had the lights of the Interlake boat in sight for a long while, and the radio call is just a formality. What is not a formality is the conversation between the MAUTHE and Algoma Marine's 730 foot motor vessel ALGOWEST, loading at the Harvest States number 1 dock, the MAUTHE's destination. Five more minutes and the ALGOWEST will vacate that dock, and head over to the Cargill B1 dock for the rest of her Seaway bound cargo. What is advantageous to the MAUTHE is that ice, three inches thick in some places, has formed within the harbor, and the ALGOWEST will break up most of it, before the Interlake boat gets there.

Passing gingerly through the cement piers of the ship canal, the MAUTHE encounters only thin, floating ice. The crunch of the ice is not heard from the bow, until the boat approaches Rices Point, where the pack is well broken up by the ALGOWEST. Around the turn at West Gate Basin, the water is open and the steamer angles in toward the dock with ease. By half past ten the MAUTHE's beam is being made fast to the Harvest States dock, but the loading shoots and crews will not work until morning. The empty steamer will wait through the night.

For more than 13 hours, grain shoots down the spouts into the Interlake boat's yawning holds. Compartments 2, 3 and 4 will receive a combined total of 480,000 bushels of Protein 14.3 at 60.4 pounds per bushel, while compartment number 1 will be filled with 141,000 bushels of Protein 15.3 at 60.5 pounds per bushel. This entire burden will give the boat a loaded draft of 22.5 feet forward, 23.1 midships and 23.8 aft. All of this raises the question "what is Protein 14.3 and 15.3, where does it come from, and what will it be used for?" If asked, the loading workers ashore and especially the crew of the MAUTHE will answer that the point is moot. It does not matter what it is, or where it comes from or even what it is to be used for—it is just grain taken at the head of the lakes that needs to be hauled to Buffalo. After this cargo they will haul another, and perhaps a couple of others, and soon the long 1992 season will be over and they will go home to their families.

After a more than 14 million bushel season, it most assuredly is "just grain."

At 11:33 p.m. Duluth time December 10th, 1992, the Interlake steamer J.L. MAUTHE slips again beneath the aerial lift bridge, and soon is well onto open Lake Superior. Noting her departure time, the wheelsmen each privately calculate the boat's estimated time at the Soo Locks, the St. Clair and Detroit rivers, and Buffalo breakwater—in an attempt to guess who will get the tough wheelin'. The Chief figures his fuel versus cargo, to get a good number for the fuel load to be taken on the next upbound stop at the Shell dock. In his room, the deck cadet works on another of the multiple projects he must complete, and down the passageway the galley staff is sound asleep (in anticipation of their normal early morning start). From the pilothouse window the captain looks out across the lake . . . and thinks about the Ohio Street turn. All around the boat, the crew is wondering how many more trips will there be this season, as the light-studded hills of Duluth-Superior fade astern.

Sunrise illuminates the boat's crew as they busy themselves hosing off the grain and dust accumulated in every corner of the vessel. Wet grain is shoveled over the side, and the rest runs from the scuppers. (The fish along the downbound route from the upper lake grain ports must be the best nourished in the world.) Thus the routine of the MAUTHE goes on all the way down to Buffalo, the only thing breaking the monotony, the emergency drill. This trip is a fire drill, cleverly timed to take place at dinner time, on the last day out. The general alarm rings, the whistle blows, the crew don lifejackets and survival suits and squirt the fire hoses over the side fore and aft, to simulate fighting a fire. (Rumor has it that on hot summer days, to break the heat, the aft crew pretends that the forward crew is afire and vice versa, thus hosing down one another.)

At long last, in the wee hours of Sunday morning, the MAUTHE is once again at the Standard Elevator, her crew preparing to start the whole routine again. To them, this whole business is not romantic or adventurous, it is just grain. It is their job . . . simply, trip 29.

Sources

JAMES SCALLON'S EMBARRASSMENT

REF Bay City Tribune, 9/11,14,15,21,26,30/1883

Cleveland Herald, 9/18,19/1883

Inland Lloyds Vessel Register, 1882

Merchant Steam Vessels of the United States, 1882

OAKLAND's Master Sheet, Institute for Great Lakes Research

THE RITES OF SPRING

REF "Namesakes 1900-1909," "1910-1919," Greenwood

"Namesakes II," Greenwood

"Great Lakes Ships We Remember," Vol. I & II, Van der Linden

Sault Saint Marie Evening News, 4/19, 21, 24, 26, 28, 30/1909; 5/1, 4/1909

The Telescope, May-June 1992, "A Classic Class" Part III, Dewar

"Freshwater Whales," Wright

Beeson's Marine Directory, 1910

Phone conversation with Tom Farnquist, 8/3/1992

ALONG PRIDGEON'S LINE

REF Saginaw Daily Courier, 9/12/1875

"History of the Great Lakes," Vol.1

Cleveland Newspaper Digest, Jan. to Dec. 1859

Chicago Inter Ocean, 9/20,22/1875

Chicago Tribune, 4/12/1869

List of Merchant Vessels of the United States, 1874

Lake Underwriters Classification, 1871,1873,1875

"Freshwater Whales," Wright

Phone conversation with Rod Danielson of Rod's Reef Diving, Ludington, MI 3/31/1992

Card catalog of the Great Lakes Historical Society, Vermillion, OH 2/21/92

"Namesakes 1900-09," Greenwood

AMONG THE JUMBLE OF KING LUMBER

REF "Great Lakes Shipwrecks and Survivals," Ratigan

"The Unholy Apostles," Keller

The American Lakes Series "Lake Superior," Nute

Bay City Daily Tribune, 9/3,13,/1881; 11/6/1881

Bay City Evening Press, 9/27,28,30/1881

Telephone conversation with Don Comtois, Essexville MI, 3/22/1992

ANTELOPE's Master Sheet, Institute for Great Lakes Research

LORD HELP 'EM ON THE LAKES TONIGHT

REF The American Lakes Series, "Lake Superior," Nute

"Shipwrecks of the Lakes," Bowen

"Namesakes 1920-29," Greenwood

Bay City Tribune, 5/3/1886; 10/2,6,8,11,12/1892

Port Huron Daily Times, 10/4,6,8,10/1892

Saginaw Courier-Herald, 10/5,7/1892

Saginaw Evening News 10/5,7/1892

NASHUA's Master Sheet, Institute for Great Lakes Research

"Freshwater Whales," Wright

DOG BARKIN'

REF Sault Saint Marie Evening News, 7/10,11/1911

Bay City Times, 7/10,11/1911

"Namesakes 1910-1911," Greenwood

"Great Lakes Ships We Remember," Vol. II, Van der Linden

The Telescope, Nov.-Dec. 1980, "Benny And The Boom," Graham

"Locks and Ships," Soo Locks Boat Tours 1989

Phone conversation with Tom Farnquist, Great Lakes Shipwreck Historical Society, 8/3/1992

AN ARCHED SHIP IN THE ICE WATER MUSEUM

REF Bay City Tribune, 9/11,14,15,21,26,30/1883

Cleveland Herald, 9/18,19/1883

Inland Lloyds Vessel Register, 1882

Merchant Steam Vessels of the United States, 1882

OAKLAND's Master Sheet, Institute for Great Lakes Research

SIGNED PATRICK HOWE

REF Oswego Daily Palladium, 10/29,30/1919

Bay City Times Tribune, 10/29,30/1919

The American Lakes Series, "Lake Huron," Landon

The American Lakes Series, "Lake Erie," Hatcher

The American Lakes Series, "Lake Superior," Nute

The American Lakes Series, "Lake Michigan," Quaife

"Namesakes 1910-1919," Greenwood

"Namesakes 1900-1909," Greenwood

"Great Lakes Ships We Remember," Vol. I & II, Van der Linden

Beeson's Marine Directory, 1920

The Telescope, Nov.-Dec. 1980, "The John S. Parsons Ship Chandlery," Palmer

Phone conversations with Terry Prior, Director, Oswego Historical Society, 6/8/1992; 11/29/1992

Phone conversation with Gretchen Rowe, 8/24/1992

Phone conversations with Lowell Nuvine, Hannable, NY Historian, 11/23,29/1992

Phone conversations with Dick Pfund and Dale Carrier of the Oswego Maritime Foundation, 11/29/1992

TROLLING FOR HISTORY

REF Cleveland Plain Dealer, 9/12/1856

Detroit Daily Democrat, 9/15/1856

Chicago Times, 3/19/1862; 3/2/1863; 2/27/1864; 4/21/1874; 11/7/1874

Cleveland Daily Herald, 3/30/1865

Chicago Republican, 4/21/1866

Toledo Blade, 3/18/1867; 7/18/1868; 10/17/1868

Chicago Tribune, 4/4/1873; 10/16,24/1876

Chicago Inter-Ocean, 4/7/1874; 10/16/1876

Port Huron Times, 11/9/1874

The Times Herald, Port Huron, MI 10/15/1989

"Freshwater Whales," Wright

"Shipwrecks of Sanilac," Pat and Jim Stayer

The Telescope, Sept.-Oct. 1978, "The Wreck of the PASSAIC," Messmer

The Telescope, Nov.-Dec. 1982 "Milwaukee and Eastern Transit Company," Middleton

The Telescope, May-June 1979 "The first PURITAN," Middleton

The American Lakes Series, "Lake Huron," Landon

The American Lakes Series, "Lake Erie," Hatcher

The American Lakes Series, "Lake Superior," Nute

The American Lakes Series, "Lake Michigan," Quaife

NEW YORK's Master Sheet, Institute for Great Lakes Research

News release, Great Lakes Shipwreck Exploration Group 10/14/1989

Abstract of enrollments, National Archives: NEW YORK, 1856

Correspondence with C. Patrick Labadie, Director, Canal Park Museum, Duluth, MN

Series of phone conversations and meetings with Jim and Pat Stayer, 1992

Proofreading and added comments on this chapter by the members of the Great Lakes Shipwreck Exploration Group, 3/1993

TRIP 29

Author's trip aboard the J. L. MAUTHE, c/o The Interlake Steamship Company and Bob Dorn.

"Freshwater Whales," Wright

The American Lakes Series, "Lake Erie," Hatcher

Buffalo Evening News, 1/21,22,23/1959

Inland Seas, Spring 1992, "The Pittsburgh Supers," Dewar

"The Fleet Histories Series," Vol.1 Greenwood

"Namesakes II," Greenwood

"Duluth-Superior, World's largest Inland Port," Van Dusen

** NOTE Persons wishing to dispute the events regarding the CASON J. CALLAWAY may view the author's unedited video tape and audio tape.*

Index of Vessels

Acknowledgements

No author works alone. The time spent "tacking away" on a computer keyboard, and spent shuffling through volumes of information is indeed a solo effort, but the struggle to get that information to the author's desk requires the investment of innumerable people. In the creation of this text I have been lucky enough to be able to lean on many people. I can say proudly that, without exception, every one that I have bothered for assistance has been most helpful and far more than kind.

What follows here is a short listing of those who, without typing a letter, helped in the production of this text.

First in the thanks must be D.J. Story, who is my eyes and ears along the Saginaw River. There often have been times when I have been stuck for a fact, and D.J. is the person that I can count on to find it in the micro film. Also, D.J. always seems to have the time, when I need someone who knows his stuff, to run to obscure places with me and help me dig up lost information. Special thanks to D.J.'s wife, Penny, for putting up with both of us—for how many wives will wait patiently on an observation platform at the Soo locks at 11:30 at night in 38 degree temperatures and nearly gale-force winds while "hubby" and his boat-nut buddy photograph and videotape the WILLOWGLEN?

Next must come the Stayers, Jim and Pat, of the Great Lakes Shipwreck Exploration Group. I will never forget the day that D.J. and I stopped by the Stayers' Lexington home and Jim greeted me with "I wanna' show you somethin'," and plopped the actual whistle from the steamer NEW YORK in my arms! (His group had petitioned the state and secured permission to bring it up—these good historians would not have it any other way.)

Thanks to Tom Farnquist of the Great Lakes Shipwreck Historical Society, who puts up with on-the-spot phone calls and gives generous and accurate information as well as taking the time to just chat. And major gratitude to Suzette Lopez of the Milwaukee Public Library who consistently is able to turn up photos of lakeboats that I never thought existed. Suzette has worked with me on all of my books and hopefully will on all to come. Thanks to Bill and Ruthann Beck of Thunder Bay Divers for sending information that can add up to at least seven chapters.

Then there is Jay Martain and Bob Graham of the Institute for Great Lakes Research who have helped me straighten out some published misinformation and present you, the readers, with the truth. Also, Chuck and Jeri Feltner and their dog Seajay who welcomed me aboard their boat GEMINI 3 as if I were an old friend. I have read their book cover to cover at least a dozen times as of today; and Dale Carrier and Dick Pfund of the newborn Oswego Maritime Foundation as well as Historian Richard Palmer, who have become my "connection" on Lake Ontario. Finally, Martha Long of the Great Lakes Historical Society, who bent the rules and let me loose in the stacks. You will be reading the results for years to come. This is just a sampling of the army of dedicated people who struggle daily to preserve and uncover the maritime heritage of the Great Lakes.

Libraries, and those who keep them in order, have been my long-distance research assistants and without their help this book would not have been possible. Peggy Lugthart of the Saginaw Public Library, Barb King of the Port Huron Public Library, Carol Ferlito of the Oswego Public Library, Ellen Bennes Gedeon of the Grand Haven Public Library, Leif Erickson of the Muskegon County Public Library, Norton Shores Branch, as well as Karla Bates also of the Muskegon Public Library, and last but without doubt, not least, Mary McManman and every one else at the Bay City Branch Library.

Now for the people who offered valuable tidbits along the way, most of whom had no idea how useful their words were. Terry Prior who is the Director of the Oswego County Historical Society, Don Comtois who, believe it or not, has made a hand-written record of about 80 percent of the vessels that have ever been into the Saginaw River (Don, get a computer). Also Marge Montgomery, Gerald Cornell, Gretchen Rowe, Ed Pusick, Gerald Cornell, Alace Saylor, Rosemary Nesbeitt, Pete Cezar, Rod Danielson, Lowell Nuvine, Jean Roe and, not to be forgotten, the Czar of lakeboat photos, Ken Thro. All of these people are a good example of why I consider the people who live in the Great Lakes region to be the friendliest on earth.

Thanks as well to Bob Dorn of the Interlake Steamship Company, and Captain Bryon Petz and the crew of the steamer J.L. MAUTHE—for putting up with this weird little guy crawling all over their boat from Buffalo to Superior and back. It is hoped that any inconvenience I may have been was worth the stories you will read.

Finally, my family—my wife Teresa, my dad Walt, mom Sue, sister Jeanine and brother Craig. Also, my gratitude to all my in-laws and in-laws to be.

To all of those I have mentioned and any I have overlooked, I thank you.

About the Author

W. Wes Oleszewski was born in Saginaw, Michigan in 1957 and grew up in the Tri-Cities area. On one particular hot summer day in 1961, Wes and his dad were strolling, pant-legs rolled up, along the shore of Lake Huron. The waves lapped at their feet as the little boy picked up every object in reach and asked the standard multitude of questions about each. Finally little Wes' attention fell upon a rough, cinder-like rock with patches of brown, black and red lodged in the light brown sand just below the water. "What's this one?" he inquired. "Probably just some iron ore," his dad casually fielded the four year old's question. "Well, how'd it get here?" the boy volleyed back. "Probably off one of them big oreboats, maybe one of 'em sank around here," his father retorted, apparently satisfying his son's curiosity for the time being. Of course there is little chance that the rock was ore and less chance that it came from a local wreck, but from that moment on Wes looked out across the deep blue lakes with an eye that visualized sunken boats and spilled cargos that were long forgotten. His interest in the Great Lakes and the oreboats that sail upon them grew up with him, watching them pass along the Saginaw River. When he started into the aviation career field in 1977, he took up Great Lakes maritime history as

a hobby. This led to the development of a personal research library, and a fleet of some 40 miniature radio-controlled oreboats. In 1982 he joined the Great Lakes Maritime Institute and later the Saginaw River Marine Historical Society, Great Lakes Historical Society and was given membership in the Great Lakes Shipwreck Historical Society.

While going through the book section of a Land and Seas maritime gift store, where he was working as a second job in Saginaw in 1986, he found that there were some relatively new books out on Great Lakes vessels, but for the most part they were just gatherings of data. Either that, or the texts involved the facts about the same two dozen or so shipwrecks. It seemed as if no one was telling the tales anymore, so Wes took it upon himself to tell the stories of the forgotten lake boats. When doing this, he decided that it was important to tell about the everyday challenges of the lakeboats, and the crews that sailed them, as well as the disasters. Every boat had a crew and every day had a story, the more obscure the better. In 1987 he finished his first book and in 1990 it was published as "Stormy Seas, Triumphs and Tragedies of Great Lakes Ships." Before the first book hit the presses he had already started work on his next, "Sounds of Disaster" and, as of this writing work, is underway on book number four.

A graduate of the Embry Riddle Aeronautical University, Wes earned a Bachelor of Science Degree in Aeronautical Science. He holds a multi-engine instrument commercial pilot's certificate and flight instructor certificates, and airline transport pilot certificate. Currently he enjoys a career as a professional pilot.